T0382605

TRANSLATIONS

TRANSLATIONS

INTO

GREEK AND LATIN VERSE

BY

Sir R. C. JEBB, Litt.D., O.M.

LATE REGIUS PROFESSOR OF GREEK IN THE UNIVERSITY OF CAMBRIDGE.

SECOND EDITION.

CAMBRIDGE :
at the University Press
1907

CAMBRIDGE
UNIVERSITY PRESS

University Printing House, Cambridge CB2 8BS, United Kingdom

Published in the United States of America by Cambridge University Press, New York

Cambridge University Press is part of the University of Cambridge.

It furthers the University's mission by disseminating knowledge in the pursuit of education, learning and research at the highest international levels of excellence.

www.cambridge.org
Information on this title: www.cambridge.org/9781107686526

First published 1907
First paperback edition 2014

A catalogue record for this publication is available from the British Library

ISBN 978-1-107-68652-6 Paperback

TO MY FATHER

PREFACE.

This book comes of a wish to gather up some work in which I have found pleasure for years.

Forty-three translations are brought together here. Thirty of these are revisions of pieces already published elsewhere. In the *Arundines Cami:* 14, 21, 22, 23, 24, 25. In the *Sertum Carthusianum:* 2, 7, 15, 16, 17, 19, 30, 31. In the *Folia Silvulae:* Part I. 3, 5, 10, 11, 13, 26, 29, 40: Part II. 4, 8, 9, 12, 18, 20, 27, 28. Leave to revise and re-print these pieces has been given by the Editor in each case.

The other thirteen translations have not been published before—1, 6, 32, 33, 34, 35, 36, 37, 38, 39, 41, 42, 43.

The metres into which I have tried to do 'Abt Vogler' are those of the fourth Pythian.

I wish to express my thanks for advice and help in preparing this book to M. Ch. Chauvet; to Dr Kennedy, Regius Professor of Greek in the University of Cambridge; to Mr F. A. Paley; and to Mr Sidney Colvin, Fellow of Trinity College and Slade Professor of Fine Art.

Trinity College, Cambridge.
        March, 1873.

PREFACE TO THE SECOND EDITION.

THIS collection of Sir Richard Jebb's compositions includes all the passages (forty-three in number) contained in the volume of 1873, with a few corrections and considerable additions. The only alteration of importance which has been made without authority is in the second line on p. 39. This line, which as originally printed was unmetrical, had been marked by Sir Richard Jebb for correction: but the alteration seems never to have been actually made. The changes in the version from Shelley (p. 83) were made by the translator himself.

The additional pieces are Macaulay's 'Epitaph on a Jacobite,' 'Polyglot Russian Scandal[1],' the Pindaric version of Leopardi's Ode on the Monument to Dante, an original Pindaric ode written for the celebration of the eighth centenary of the University of Bologna; also a translation in Pindaric metre of a poem by Mr Rann Kennedy, father of the late Professor B. H. Kennedy, who printed it in his volume entitled 'Between Whiles' (Bell, 1877). It is here reproduced by permission of the Misses Kennedy. Finally, for the hitherto unprinted version which stands last in the book the editor is indebted to the kindness of Mr Alfred Pretor, Fellow of St Catharine's.

R. D. A. H.

February 1907.

---

[1] The original verses from which this set of translations was made were written by the late W. G. Clark. The English was done into Latin, the Latin into Greek, and so forth; the last translation being done again into English: thus only the Latin translator saw the original verses. It looks as if only the latter half of Mr Clark's poem has survived: since not only is the Latin version twice the length of the English as here printed, but the first four lines stand in no discernible relation to it. However this may be, the editor has not succeeded in tracing any more lines.

CONTENTS.

CONTENTS.

ABT VOGLER.

WOULD that the structure brave, the manifold music I build,
  Bidding my organ obey, calling its keys to their work,
Claiming each slave of the sound, at a touch, as when
    Solomon willed
  Armies of angels that soar, legions of demons that lurk,
Man, brute, reptile, fly,—alien of end and of aim,
  Adverse, each from the other heaven-high, hell-deep re-
    moved,—
Should rush into sight at once as he named the ineffable
    Name,
  And pile him a palace straight, to pleasure the princess
    he loved!

ΥΜΝΟΣ.

εἴθε μίμνοι ποικιλόφωνον ἔδος,   στροφή.

δῶμ᾽ ὃ τεύχω δαιδαλόεν, καλέσαις αὐλῶν κλυτὰν πειθάνορ᾽ ὑπη-
    ρεσίαν,

πρόσπολ᾽ ὄρσαις φθέγμαθ᾽ ἕτοιμα θιγών, ὡς δαιμόνων ὄρσεν
    ποτανὰν

οὐρανίων τε βίαν Σολόμων καὶ ταρταρείων,

ἄνδρα τε θῆρά τε μυῖάν θ᾽ ἕρπετόν τ᾽, ἐναντίους

ἔργον ἀλλάλοις μέριμνάν τ᾽, οὐρανὸς ὡς ἐρέβευς, προθορεῖν,

ὡς κρέοντ᾽ αὔδασ᾽ ἀναύδατον, φίλας αἰρέμεν

δόμον ἄφαρ μείλιγμ᾽ ἀνάσσας·

Would it might tarry like his, the beautiful building of mine,
  This which my keys in a crowd pressed and importuned
    to raise!
Ah, one and all, how they helped, would dispart now and
    now combine,
  Zealous to hasten the work, heighten their master his praise!
And one would bury his brow with a blind plunge down
    to hell,
  Burrow awhile and build, broad on the roots of things,
Then up again swim into sight, having based me my
    palace well,
  Founded it, fearless of flame, flat on the nether springs.

And another would mount and march, like the excellent
    minion he was,
  Ay, another and yet another, one crowd but with many
    a crest,
Raising my rampired walls of gold as transparent as glass,
  Eager to do and die, yield each his place to the rest:
For higher still and higher (as a runner tips with fire,
  When a great illumination surprises a festal night—
Outlining round and round Rome's dome from space to spire)
  Up, the pinnacled glory reached, and the pride of my
    soul was in sight.

εἴθε μοι τοῖον μένοι ἱμερόεν   ἀντιστροφή.

δῶμ᾽ ὃ παμφώνοισιν ἀολλέες ἠπείγονθ᾽ ἁμίλλαις χόρδαι ἐποικο-
     δομεῖν·

ὡς ἕκασται συμπόνεον, σποράδαν εἶτ᾽ ἰλαδόν, πρόθυμοι

δεσπότου ἔργον ἐπουρίσαι εὔκλειάν τ᾽ ἐπαίρειν·

κᾆθ᾽ ὁ μὲν ἐς δνοφερὸν πρανὴς κολυμβῶν Τάρταρον

γᾶς πλατείας ἀμφὶ ῥίζας σκάπτε τέως πονέων κέλαδος,

εἶτ᾽ ἀνᾷσσ᾽, εὖ δῶμά μοι παγὰν κτίσας νερτερᾶν

πυρὸς ἀθίκτοις ἐν θεμέθλοις·

ἄλλος αὖ σύν τ᾽ ἄλλος ἄνω βεβαώς, θαυμαστὰ λατρεύων
     στρατὸς   ἐπῳδός.

εἷς ἑκατογκεφάλας, πάγχρυσον ἦρεν λαμπροτέρων ὑάλου

ἔρμα πύργων, δρᾶν τι πᾶς τις καὶ θανέμεν μεμαώς,

τῷ πέλας εἴκων· ὡς γὰρ εὖτ᾽ ἔκρηξ᾽ ἀφράστου φέγγεα παννυχίδος,

θεῖ τις πυρὶ βυσσόθεν ἐς κορυφὰν τηλαυγὲς ἱρὸν

ἐκστέφων Ῥώμας ἄωτον, τοῖον ἀεὶ

καλλιπύργου θαύματος αἰρομένου χάρμα μοι ψυχᾶς ἐφάνθη·

In sight? Not half! for it seemed, it was certain, to match
    man's birth,
  Nature in turn conceived, obeying an impulse as I;
And the emulous heaven yearned down, made effort to
    reach the earth,
  As the earth had done her best, in my passion, to scale
    the sky:
Novel splendours burst forth, grew familiar and dwelt with mine,
  Not a point nor peak but found and fixed its wandering star;
Meteor-moons, balls of blaze: and they did not pale nor pine,
  For earth had attained to heaven, there was no more
    near nor far.

Nay more; for there wanted not who walked in the glare
    and glow,
  Presences plain in the place; or, fresh from the Protoplast,
Furnished for ages to come, when a kindlier wind should blow,
  Lured now to begin and live, in a house to their liking at last;
Or else the wonderful Dead who have passed through the
    body and gone,
  But were back once more to breathe in an old world
    worth their new:
What never had been, was now; what was, as it shall be anon;
  And what is,—shall I say, matched both? for I was
    made perfect too.

ἀλλὰ μὰν οὐδ' ἄμισύ πω κάτιδον· *στροφή.*

τίκτε γὰρ δὴ χἀ Φύσις ἀντιπάλους θναταῖσι βλαστὰς ἶσ' ἐμοὶ
αὐτόματος,

καὶ χθόν' αἰθὴρ προσκύσαι ἀντεράων ὠρέξατ' ὀργαίνων ἄνωθεν,

οἷα καὶ αἰθέρ' ἐμαῖς ἀναβᾶμεν γαῖ' ἐν ὁρμαῖς·

φέγγεα δ' ἁμετέροις ἀλλοῖα μίχθη συντρόφως,

πᾶν τ' ἀκρὸν μήνας τε λάμπας τ', ἄστρα πλανήτ', ἔχ' ἐφεζομένας·

οὐδ' ἐτείρονθ'· ὡς γὰρ ἤδη γᾶς πόλονδ' ἰγμένας

τό τε πρόσω ταὐτὸν τό τ' ἐγγύς.

ἦν δὲ καὶ πρὸς τοῖσδέ τιν' εἰσοράαν *ἀντιστροφή.*

ἐντόπων πάμπρεπτα πρόσωπα πυριφλέκτοις ἀναστρωφώμεν' ἐν
ἀγλαΐαις·

εἶτ' ἐπ' αἰῶν' οὔρια πνευσόμενον θείοις νεοκτίστους τύποισιν

καινίσαι ἄρτι βίον δόμος ἁρμοῖ θέλξ' ἑαδώς·

εἴτε διαπταμένων σεμνὰν νεκρῶν ὁμήγυριν

πεῖσ' ἀνελθεῖν τἀνθάδ' ἶσα τοῖς ἐκεῖ· ἦν γὰρ ἃ πρὶν μὲν ἀπῆν,

πρὶν δ' ὅσ' ἦν, ἦν οἷ' ἔτ' ἔσται· τοῖς δ', ὅσ' ἔστ', ἤρισε·

τέλεα γὰρ καὶ τἀμάγ', εἰπεῖν.

All through my keys that gave their sounds to a wish of
  my soul,
  All through my soul that praised as its wish flowed
    visibly forth,
All through music and me! For think, had I painted the whole,
  Why, there it had stood, to see, nor the process so won-
    der-worth:
Had I written the same, made verse—still, effect proceeds
  from cause,
  Ye know why the forms are fair, ye hear how the tale is told;
It is all triumphant art, but art in obedience to laws,
  Painter and poet are proud in the artist-list enrolled:—

But here is the finger of God, a flash of the will that can,
  Existent behind all laws, that made them and, lo, they are!
And I know not if, save in this, such gift be allowed to man,
  That out of three sounds he frame, not a fourth sound,
    but a star.
Consider it well: each tone of our scale in itself is nought;
  It is everywhere in the world—loud, soft, and all is said:
Give it to me to use! I mix it with two in my thought
  And, there! Ye have heard and seen: consider and bow
    the head!

πᾶν τόδ᾽ αὐλῶν τ᾽ ἔργον, ἐμᾶς κελαδησάντων κατ᾽ εὐχωλὰν
    φρενός,   ἐπῳδός.
καὶ φρενὸς ἃ νοέοισ᾽ εὐχὰν ἀνευφάμασ᾽ ἐπιτελλομέναν,
χάρμ᾽ ἐμοὶ κείνοισί τ᾽· εἰ γὰρ τεῦξα γραφαῖς τάδ᾽, ἰδὼν
τίς κεν ἀγάσθη μαχανάν; εἰ δ᾽ ἐν πτυχαῖς ᾤκισ᾽ ὕμνων, ὅ τε δρῶν
δῆλος τό τε δρᾶμ᾽· ὅθεν ἐστὶ καλὸν σχῆμ᾽, ἴσθ᾽, ὅ τ᾽ αἶνος
οἷα λέξ᾽· ὡρισμένας ταῦτ᾽ ἆθλα τέχνας·
ἐς τεχνίτας γὰρ τελέειν, τόδ᾽ ἀοιδοῖς κλέος καὶ ζωγράφοισιν·

νῦν δὲ δαίμων ἐξεκάλυψε βίαν,   στροφή.
ἀστραπὰν ὥς, παντοπόρου κραδίας, θεσμῶν κνεφαῖον τέκτον᾽
    ἀριπρεπέων·
ποῦ γὰρ ἐξῆν ἄλλο βροτοῖς τι τοιόνδ᾽, οἷον κτύπους τρεῖς συμ-
    πλάσαντι
μὴ τέτρατον κτύπον ἀλλὰ σέλας πάμφλεκτον αἴρειν;
αὐτό τοι ἁρμονίας φώναμ᾽ ἕκαστον εὐτελές,
δαμόθρουν, μέγ᾽ εἴτε λεπτόν, ῥῆμ᾽ ἁπλόον· τὸ δ᾽ ἐγὼ κεράσας
σὺν δυοῖν ἄλλοις τί τεῦξ᾽; ἠκούσατ᾽, εἴδετε·
θέσκελον θαυμάζετ᾽ ἀλκάν.

Well, it is gone at last, the palace of music I reared;
  Gone! and the good tears start, the praises that come
    too slow;
For one is assured at first, one scarce can say that he feared,
  That he even gave it a thought, the gone thing was to go.
Never to be again! But many more of the kind
  As good, nay, better perchance: is this your comfort to me?
To me, who must be saved because I cling with my mind
  To the same, same self, same love, same God: ay, what
    was, shall be.

Therefore to whom turn I but to Thee, the ineffable Name?
  Builder and maker, Thou, of houses not made with hands!
What, have fear of change from Thee who art ever the same?
  Doubt that Thy power can fill the heart that Thy power
    expands?
There shall never be one lost good! What was, shall live
    as before;
  The evil is null, is nought, is silence implying sound;
What was good, shall be good, with, for evil, so much
    good more;
  On the earth, the broken arcs; in the heaven, a perfect
    round.

εἶεν, οἴχει δή, πολύχορδον ἕδος,   ἀντιστροφή.

δακρύων τ᾽ ἔρρωγ᾽ ἐπ᾽ ὀλωλότι χλωρὸν δεῦμα παιάν τ᾽ ὀψέ περ

    ὀρνύμενος·

ἠρχόμην γὰρ θαρσαλέως, ἔτυμ᾽ εἰπεῖν, οὔτε δείσας οὔτε δηχθείς,

τοῦδ᾽ ὃ βέβακεν ὁδὸν προνοήσας μοιρόκραντον·

τοῦτο μὲν οὐκέτ᾽ ἄρ᾽ ἔστ᾽· ἔσται δὲ δῆθεν ἀλλ᾽ ἴσα

κἄτι κρείσσω. ψυχρὰ θρυλεῖς. οὐ γὰρ ἐὼν ἐγὼ αὐτὸς ἀεί,

ταὐτά τ᾽ αἰὲν πατρὶ σὺν ταὐτῷ σέβων, σώζομαι;

ὅσα πάροιθ᾽ ἦν, φαμ᾽ ἔσεσθαι.

ποῖον οὖν εἰ μὴ σέγ᾽, ἐπωνυμίαν ἄρρητον ὠνομασμένε,   ἐπῳδός.

προστρέπομαι, μελάθρων χείρεσσιν οὐ τεκταινομένων γενέτωρ;

ἄστροφος πῶς ὢν στραφήσει; πῶς κέαρ ἀμπετάσας

οὐ κορέσεις; οὐδὲν θανεῖται χρηστόν· ἐσλὰ ζήσει ἔθ᾽ ὅσσα

    πρὶν ἦν·

σιγῶν δ᾽ ἀγαθὸν τὸ κακόν, πλέον οὐδέν. χρήστ᾽ ἔτ᾽ ἔσται

πάνθ᾽ ὅσ᾽ ἦν, τόσσοις σὺν ἄλλοις ἀντὶ κακῶν·

γαῖα μὲν γὰρ κῶλα ῥαγέντα κύκλου, Ζεὺς δ᾽ ὁρᾷ κύκλον τέλειον.

All we have willed or hoped or dreamed of good, shall exist;
  Not its semblance, but itself; no beauty, nor good, nor
    power
Whose voice has gone forth, but each survives for the
    melodist
When eternity affirms the conception of an hour.
The high that proved too high, the heroic for earth too hard,
  The passion that left the ground to lose itself in the sky,
Are music sent up to God by the lover and the bard;
  Enough that he heard it once: we shall hear it by-and-by.

And what is our failure here but a triumph's evidence
  For the fulness of the days?   Have we withered or
    agonized?
Why else was the pause prolonged but that singing might
    issue thence?
  Why rushed the discords in, but that harmony should be
    prized?
Sorrow is hard to bear, and doubt is slow to clear,
  Each sufferer says his say, his scheme of the weal and woe:
But God has a few of us whom he whispers in the ear;
  The rest may reason and welcome: 't is we musicians know.

πάνθ' ἃ βουλαῖς ἐλπίσι τ' ἐπλάσαμεν   στροφή.

χρήστ', ὀνείροις τ', ἔσσεται, οὐ δοκέοντ' ἀλλ' αὐτά· κεδνὸν πᾶν
     σθεναρόν τ' ἐρατόν θ',

οὗ γ' ἅπαξ φωνὰ κελάδησε, μένει τοῖσι φωνήσασιν, εὖτε

κραίνει ἐφημερίων ὑπονοίας πλεῖστος αἰών.

ὑψίφρον εἴ τι λίαν, εἰ θέσκελον φάνη βροτοῖς,

εἰ δ' ἔρως τις γᾶν προλείπων πλάζετ' ἐπ' αἰθέρ', ἔπεμψε θεῷ

τοῦτ' ἐραστὴς φθέγμ' ἀοιδός τ'· εἰ δ' ἅπαξ ᾔσθετο

θεός, ἀκούοιμέν κ' ἔτ' ἄνδρες.

εἰ δὲ νῦν ἐσφάλμεθ', ἐπαγγελία   ἀντιστροφή.

τοῦτο νίκας ἅμασι σὺν τελέοις. ἠθλήσαμέν που πολλὰ μαραι-
     νόμενοι·

ἀλλ' ἀναύδου μῆνες ἀμαχανίας πῶς οὐχ ὕμνους μέλλουσι τίκτειν,

καὶ πόθον ἁρμονίας ἐπιβᾶσαι πλημμέλειαι;

δύσφορός ἐστιν ἀνία δύσλυτόν τε τἀσαφές·

πᾶς δέ τις τό τ' εὖ ῥυθμίζων καὶ τὸ κακὸν λαλέει νοσέων·

ἔστι δ' οἷς φράζει δι' ὠτὸς Ζεύς· σκοπεῖθ', ἅτεροι·

φαμὲν ἐπίστασθαι μελῳδοί.

Well, it is earth with me; silence resumes her reign :
  I will be patient and proud, and soberly acquiesce.
Give me the keys.   I feel for the common chord again,
  Sliding by semitones, till I sink to the minor,—yes,
And I blunt it into a ninth, and I stand on alien ground,
  Surveying awhile the heights I rolled from into the deep ;
Which, hark, I have dared and done, for my resting-place
    is found,
  The C Major of this life : so, now I will try to sleep.

BROWNING.

εἶεν· ἐξάλλαξα πάλιν χθαμαλὸς σιγὰν βρέμοντος οὐρανοῦ· ἐπῳδός.
τλάσομαι ὑψιφρόνως.   χορδῶν, φέρ᾽, ὄρσαις ἀρχέτυπον κέλαδον,
βαθμίσιν φωνῶν πολυξέστοισι καθιέμενος,
κλίνομαι εἰς ἀμβλύν τιν᾽ ἆχον, τοῦ πρὶν ἐκβὰς τέρμ᾽· ἄγαμαι
    δὲ τέως
ὕμνων κορυφὰς ἆλ᾽ ὅθεν κατενέχθην εἰς ἄπειρον·
ἀμπνέω δὴ τλὰς τόδ᾽ ἔρδειν· πλᾶξα μέσαν,
ἐλπίδων κρηπῖδα βροτοῖς βιότου· νῦν δ᾽ ὕπνον γένοιτ᾽ ἰαύειν.

TITHONUS.

THE woods decay, the woods decay and fall,
The vapours weep their burthen to the ground,
Man comes and tills the field and lies beneath,
And after many a summer dies the swan.
Me only cruel immortality
Consumes : I wither slowly in thine arms,
Here at the quiet limit of the world,
A white-hair'd shadow roaming like a dream
The ever silent spaces of the East,
Far-folded mists, and gleaming halls of morn.

TITHONUS.

Marcescunt nemorum, nemorum labuntur honores,

roriferae deflent nubes, oriuntur et arvis

incumbunt subterque hominum defuncta recumbunt

saecla, nec aestates non deciduntur oloris.

solus ego immortale trahens aegerrimus aevom

carpor: inaresco, te complectente, quietum

limen ad hoc mundi, dum cana remetior umbra

secretas orientis imagine vanior aulas,

multiplices nebulas, sublustria templa diei.

J. T.

Alas! for this gray shadow, once a man—
So glorious in his beauty and thy choice,
Who madest him thy chosen, that he seem'd
To his great heart none other than a God!
I ask'd thee, 'Give me immortality.'
Then didst thou grant mine asking with a smile,
Like wealthy men who care not how they give.
But thy strong Hours indignant work'd their wills,
And beat me down and marr'd and wasted me,
And though they could not end me, left me maim'd
To dwell in presence of immortal youth,
Immortal age beside immortal youth,
And all I was, in ashes. Can thy love,
Thy beauty, make amends, though even now,
Close over us, the silver star, thy guide,
Shines in those tremulous eyes that fill with tears
To hear me? Let me go: take back thy gift:
Why should a man desire in any way
To vary from the kindly race of men,
Or pass beyond the goal of ordinance

heu senis hanc umbram, prius e terrestribus unum

quom specie florens et te dignante cubili,

dignabaris enim, quicquid sublime minatus

quin darer in superos adeo nil rebar abesse!

concilies, dixi, caelum mihi.   blanda roganti

annuis: haud aliter terrae quoque plenior heres

largirique solet nec habere quod imputet illud.

sed rabiem explerunt ultrices acriter Horae

et stravere graves et mutavere terendo,

quodque necem citra poterant, deformis adessem

aeternae voluere iuventutique senectus

divinae divina, meae facis ipse superstes.

num vel amor tanti, pulcerrima? sidere quanquam

dum loquor impendente, tuae duce lampadis albo,

suave coruscantes oculi miserantis abortis

stant lacrimis?   absolve, precor, retro exime donum.

cur velit humani generis transcendere quoquam

foedus homo aut sanctos ultra procedere fines?

2—2

Where all should pause, as is most meet for all?

A soft air fans the cloud apart; there comes
A glimpse of that dark world where I was born.
Once more the old mysterious glimmer steals
From thy pure brows, and from thy shoulders pure,
And bosom beating with a heart renew'd.
Thy cheek begins to redden through the gloom,
Thy sweet eyes brighten slowly close to mine,
Ere yet they blind the stars, and the wild team
Which love thee, yearning for thy yoke, arise,
And shake the darkness from their loosen'd manes,
And beat the twilight into flakes of fire.

Lo! ever thus thou growest beautiful
In silence, then before thine answer given
Departest, and thy tears are on my cheek.

Why wilt thou ever scare me with thy tears,
And make me tremble lest a saying learnt,
In days far off, on that dark earth, be true?
'The Gods themselves cannot recall their gifts.'

Ay me! ay me! with what another heart,

hic cunctis claudenda, hic clausa probabitur aetas.

   intremuit zephyro nubes : hiemale meorum

nosco exul litus, senis incunabula nosco.

ecce tuo miror de vertice lumen oriri,

miror ab ambrosio non enarrabile collo,

miror rite novam sumentia pectora vitam.

iamque tepere genas sensim et splendescere cerno

instantis dulces oculos, necdum orbibus illi

astra hebetant plenis, necdum exultantia fervent

corda reposcentum sibi quae moderetur equorum,

effunduntque iubas ut opaca volumina currus

discutiat tenebrarum insultetque ignifer umbris.

   en tua te quoties inter mea vota venustas

induit, expectans quid responsura moreris

deseror et lacrimis astans umector euntis.

   quo lacrimis me usque exanimas? quo me usque timentem

ne sit verum, angis, quod egeno lucis in aevo

nocte laborantum memini portendere famam,

ipsos, quae dederint, non posse resumere divos?

   hei mihi, quam non his oculis Tithonus inhaerens,

In days far off, and with what other eyes
I used to watch—if I be he that watch'd—
The lucid outline forming round thee; saw
The dim curls kindle into sunny rings;
Changed with thy mystic change, and felt my blood
Glow with the glow that slowly crimson'd all
Thy presence and thy portals, while I lay,
Mouth, forehead, eyelids, growing dewy-warm
With kisses balmier than half-opening buds
Of April, and could hear the lips that kiss'd
Whispering I knew not what of wild and sweet,
Like that strange song I heard Apollo sing,
While Ilion like a mist rose into towers.

Yet hold me not for ever in thine East:
How can my nature longer mix with thine?
Coldly thy rosy shadows bathe me, cold
Are all thy lights, and cold my wrinkled feet
Upon thy glimmering thresholds, when the steam
Floats up from those dim fields about the homes
Of happy men that have the power to die,

ille ego si spiro, quam non hoc corde tuebar

gliscere te cingens iubar et pallentis apricos

stare comis cirros miramque subire videbar

te subeunte vicem, penitus magis ossa calescens

quo portae magis et rubor ardescebat obortae!

at tua labra mihi crebrum irrorantia nectar

os frontemque dabant resupino et lumina circum

oscula quis vernae non germina suavius halant

semireducta rosae; nec secius oscula figens

nescio quid clementis inexpertique canebas.

crescere sic Phoebi plusquam mortale recordor

carmen, at in turres nebulosam assurgere Troiam.

ne tamen aeternum his claustris orientis in aevom

saepiar: an leti fruar immortalibus heres

amplius? en roseis involvor frigidus umbris,

frigida candescunt tua limina, friget eoum

sub pede rugato limen, cum mane vapores

submittunt procul obscuro cingentia tractu

arva domos hominum, quis posse perire beatis

And grassy barrows of the happier dead.

Release me, and restore me to the ground ;

Thou seest all things, thou wilt see my grave :

Thou wilt renew thy beauty morn by morn ;

I earth in earth forget these empty courts,

And thee returning on thy silver wheels.

TENNYSON.

contigit aut fato caespes potiore sepultis.

da moriar, da reddar humo : tu cetera lustras,

tu senis agnosces tumulum : reparabis honorem

tu, dea, quot redeunt luces : me terra recondet

terrenum : per me sileant haec templa licebit

tuque albis volvare revolvarisque quadrigis.

SONG.

HOME they brought her warrior dead :
  She nor swoon'd, nor utter'd cry :
All her maidens, watching, said,
  'She must weep or she will die.'

Then they praised him, soft and low,
  Call'd him worthy to be loved,
Truest friend and noblest foe ;
  Yet she neither spoke nor moved.

CARMEN.

Mortuus e bello sua fertur in atria miles :
   nec fluit ad terram sponsa nec ore gemit :
aspiciunt unaque canunt haec voce puellae ;
   a ! fleat—est lacrimis, ne moriatur, opus.
inde viri repetunt summisso murmure laudes :
   dignus erat, narrant, quem sequeretur amor,
fidus amicitiis, ipsos generosus in hostes ;
   illa tamen nullos dat stupefacta sonos.

Stole a maiden from her place,
  Lightly to the warrior stept,
Took the face-cloth from the face ;
  Yet she neither moved nor wept.

Rose a nurse of ninety years,
  Set his child upon her knee—
Like summer tempest came her tears—
  'Sweet my child, I live for thee.'

TENNYSON.

provenit e mediis elapsa puella ministris,

    fert levis ad feretrum qua iacet ille pedem ;

dimovet a rigido feralem sindona voltu :

    illa tamen siccis torpet ut ante genis.

surgit anus denos novies emensa Decembres ;

    in gremium pignus dat puerile viri :

imber ut aestivos rupit pia lacrima fontes ;

    tu, puer, in vita cur morer, inquit, eris.

WORCESTER. HOTSPUR. NORTHUMBERLAND.

WOR.   Peace, cousin, say no more!
          And now I will unclasp a secret book,
          And to your quick-conceiving discontents
          I'll read you matter deep and dangerous,
          As full of peril and adventurous spirit
          As to o'er-walk a current roaring loud
          On the unsteadfast footing of a spear.
HOT.   If he fall in, good night! or sink or swim:
          Send danger from the east unto the west,

ΑΝΑΚΤΕΣ. ΘΡΑΣΥΜΑΧΟΣ.

ΑΝΑΞ Α. εὔφημον, ὦ ξύναιμε, κοίμισον στόμα·
δέλτου δ᾽ ἀνοίξας νῦν ἀπορρήτους πτυχὰς
πρὸς μανθάνειν φθάνοντας ὡς δεδηγμένους
μελαμβαθές τι πρᾶγος ἐξηγήσομαι,
θερμοῦ θ᾽ ὁμοίως κἀπικινδύνου θράσους
ὥσπερ χάρυβδιν ἐκπερᾶν βαρύβρομον
δορὸς γεφυρωθεῖσαν ἀστάτῳ βάσει.

ΘΡΑΣ. ἴτω γ᾽ ὁ πίπτων· νεῖν γὰρ ἢ θανεῖν ἀκμή·
ἀπ᾽ ἀντολῶν τὸ δεινὸν ἐς δυσμὰς ἄφες,

So honour cross it from the north to south,

And let them grapple: O, the blood more stirs

To rouse a lion than to start a hare!

NORTH. Imagination of some great exploit

Drives him beyond the bounds of patience.

HOT. By heaven, methinks it were an easy leap

To pluck bright honour from the pale-faced moon,

Or dive into the bottom of the deep,

Where fathom-line could never touch the ground,

And pluck up drowned honour by the locks;

So he that doth redeem her thence might wear

Without corrival all her dignities:

But out upon this half-faced fellowship!

SHAKESPEARE.

ἢν γ᾽ ἀνταφῇς βορράθεν ἐς νότον κλέος,
τὼ δ᾽ οὖν ἀμιλλάσθωσαν· ὡς ἀνεπτάμην
λέοντ᾽ ἐγείρων μᾶλλον ἢ φοβῶν πτάκα.

ΑΝΑΞ Β. ἔοικεν ἀνὴρ ἔνθεος λαμπροῦ τινὸς
ἔργου φέρεσθαι τοῦ φρονεῖν ἔξω δραμών.

Θ. ὦ θεοί, τόδ᾽ ὡς πήδημ᾽ ἂν εὐχερῶς δοκῶ
πηδῶν σελήνης ἁρπάσαι τ᾽ εὐδοξίαν
χρυσῶπ᾽ ἀπ᾽ ἀργυρῶπος, ἔς τε ποντίους
βυθοὺς κολυμβῶν ἔνθα μὴ κέλσει στάθμη
κομῶν κατακλυσθεῖσαν ἐξανασπάσαι,
ἐφ᾽ ᾧ τὸν ἐκσώσαντα τὴν παμπησίαν
τιμῆς ἄλυπον τοῦ μεθέξοντος φορεῖν·
ἡ δ᾽ ἀμφίλεκτος ἐρρέτω κοινωνία.

THE DYING SWAN.

THE wild swan's death-hymn took the soul
Of that waste place with joy
Hidden in sorrow: at first to the ear
The warble was low, and full and clear;
And floating about the under sky,
Prevailing in weakness, the coronach stole
Sometimes afar, and sometimes anear;
But anon her awful jubilant voice,
With a music strange and manifold,
Flow'd forth on a carol free and bold;

OLOR MORIENS.

Quae loca ferali penitus dulcedine cantus

cepit olor moriens. primo summissa venire

murmura plorantis liquidoque arguta susurro,

dum vaga depressis humili sub nubibus ala

grassatur trepidando aut longe nenia serpens

aut propior: sed mox plenum increbrescere carmen

morte triumphantis, graviorque in sidera paean

mille rapi numeris et gloria fervere cantus:

3—2

As when a mighty people rejoice

With shawms and with cymbals, and harps of gold,

And the tumult of their acclaim is roll'd

Thro' the open gates of the city afar,

To the shepherd who watcheth the evening star.

And the creeping mosses and clambering weeds,

And the willow-branches hoar and dank,

And the wavy swell of the soughing reeds,

And the wave-worn horns of the echoing bank,

And the silvery marish-flowers that throng

The desolate creeks and pools among,

Were flooded over with eddying song.

TENNYSON.

qualis ubi magno in populo si tympana festum

mixta tubis celebrant citharisque sonatur et auro

it strepitus portis, et ovantia murmura volvi

vesperis exaudit tremulo sub lumine pastor.

iamque comas muscorum humiles herbaeque sequacis

gramina, iam canis saliceta madentia ramis,

quaeque terunt fluctus resonantis cornua ripae,

quaeque sinus vastos desolatasque paludes

innumero decorant argentea lilia coetu,

obruit exundans numeroso gurgite carmen.

Silence.

THEY seem'd to those who saw them meet
The worldly friends of every day:
Her smile was undisturbed and sweet,
His courtesy was free and gay:
But yet, if one the other's name
In some unguarded moment heard,
The heart you thought so calm and tame,
Would struggle like a captur'd bird;
And letters of mere formal phrase
Were blister'd with repeated tears.

Silebant.

Verba serunt isti, poteras conviva putare,
  convivae volgo qualia forte serunt :
illa nihil trepidum, nil triste prementis ad instar
  ridet ; in urbanos par vacat ille sales.
si tamen alterius non praevigilantis ad aurem
  alterius nomen vox inopina tulit,
tam, reor, apta iugo, tam scilicet inscia flammae
  corda micant qualis capta columba micat :
quaeque salutantis frigebat epistola nugis
  plus semel affusa tabuerat lacrima.

And this was not the work of days,

But had gone on for years and years.

Alas, that Love was not too strong

For maiden shame and manly pride!

Alas, that they delay'd so long

The goal of mutual bliss beside!

Yet, what no chance could then reveal,

And neither would be first to own,

Let fate and courage now conceal,

When truth could bring remorse alone.

LORD HOUGHTON.

nec brevium spatio mens venerat illa dierum ;
    creverat annorum lentus amaror opus.
digna viro gravitas pudor o si virgine dignus
    obstabant, utinam praevaluisset amor !
o utinam voti stantes iam fine sub ipso
    ivissent positis quo voluere moris !
quod tamen haud usquam fors tempestiva reclusit,
    quodque prior fari segnis uterque fuit,
id sua fata tegant, id fortia corda recondant,
    ne pigeat frustra dissimulata loqui.

FEDALMA.   ZARCA.

No, no—I will not say it—I will go!
Father, I choose!   I will not take a heaven
Haunted by shrieks of far-off misery.
This deed and I have ripened with the hours:
It is a part of me—a wakened thought
That, rising like a giant, masters me,
And grows into a doom.   O mother life,
That seemed to nourish me so tenderly,
Even in the womb you vowed me to the fire,
Hung on my soul the burden of men's hopes,
And pledged me to redeem.—I'll pay the debt!
You gave me strength that I should pour it all

ΦΕΙΔΑΛΜΗ. ΞΑΡΚΗΣ.

Φ. μὴ δῆτ'· ἐρῶ τόδ' οὔποτ'· ἀλλ' ἅμ' ἕψομαι.
πάτερ, δέδοκται· μηδ' ἴση ζῴην θεοῖς
φρίσσουσα κωκυτοῖσιν ἐκτόπου δύης.
ἐμοὶ γὰρ ἔργον συντρόφως τόδ' ἤκμασεν
ὡς συμπεφυκός· οὗ μέλημ' ἐγρηγορὸς
γίγας τις ὣς πάνταρχον αἴρεται φρενῶν,
δίκην ἀνάγκης βρῖθον· ὦ ζωῆς γάνος
μητρῷον, ὦ δόξασά μ' ἠπίως τρέφειν,
κἂν γαστρί μ' οὖσαν πῦρ ἄρ' ὥρισας περᾶν,
ψυχῆς δ' ἀπαρτῶσ' ἐλπίδας πολλῶν μιᾶς
τελεῖν κατηγγύησας· ὥσπερ οὖν τελῶ.
σθένος γὰρ εἶ μοι δοῦσ' ἵν' ἐγχέαιμι πᾶν

Into this anguish.   I can never shrink

Back into bliss—my heart has grown too big

With things that might be.   Father, I will go.

O Father, will the women of our tribe

Suffer as I do in the years to come

When you have made them great in Africa?

Redeemed from ignorant ills only to feel

A conscious woe?   Then—is it worth the pains?

Were it not better when we reach that shore

To raise a funeral pile and perish all?

So closing up a myriad avenues

To misery yet unwrought?   My soul is faint—

Will these sharp pains buy any certain good?

    Zarca.   Nay, never falter: no great deed is done

By falterers who wish for certainty.

No good is certain, but the steadfast mind,

The undivided will to seek the good:

The greatest gift the hero leaves his race,

Is to have been a hero.

                        GEORGE ELIOT.

εἰς τήνδ᾽ ἀνίαν· οὐδ᾽ ἂν εἰς στενὴν χαρὰν
θυμὸν κατισχνάναιμ᾽ ἔτ᾽ ἐξωγκωμένον
ἔρωτι τοῦ μέλλοντος· ἕψομαι, πάτερ.
ἢ χἀτέραις, γεννῆτορ, ἐμφύλων μένει
ἐμοῖς ἴσ᾽ ἀντλεῖν καὶ μεταῦθις ἄλγεσιν,
ἑδρῶν κρατούσαις, σὴν δόσιν, Λιβυστικῶν ;
ἐξ ἀγνοουσῶν ἢ ξυνειδυίαις τρέφειν
λύπας πάρεσται ; κᾷτα δρᾶν προὔργου τάδε ;
οὐ κρεῖσσον ἀκτὴν ἱγμένοις Λιβυστικὴν
κοινῇ πυρὰν νήσασιν ἐξολωλέναι,
ἀνηρίθμους εἴρξασι προσβολὰς κακῶν
μήπω φανέντων ; φεῦ· φρέν᾽ ὡς βαρύνομαι·
μῶν κέρδος ὠδὶς ἐμπολᾷ πικρὰ σαφές ;

Ξ. μή νυν ὀκνήσῃς μηδέν· ὡς ὅσοι σαφῆ
ποθοῦντες ὀκνοῦσ᾽ οὐδὲν αἴρονται μέγα.
σαφὲς γὰρ ἀγαθὸν φρὴν ἀκίνητος μόνον,
σπουδῇ τ᾽ ἀκραιφνὴς τἀγάθ᾽ ἐξιχνοσκοπεῖν.
λείπει δ᾽ ὁ δράσας λαμπρὰ τοῖς ἐμφυλίοις
τοῦτ᾽ αὐτὸ λῷστον, λαμπρὰ καὶ δεδρακέναι.

Dost thou look back?

Dost thou look back on what hath been,
 As some divinely-gifted man,
 Whose life in low estate began
And on a simple village green ;

Who breaks his birth's invidious bar,
 And grasps the skirts of happy chance,
 And breasts the blows of circumstance,
And grapples with his evil star:

Who makes by force his merit known,
 And lives to clutch the golden keys,
 To mould a mighty state's decrees,
And shape the whisper of the throne:

Ut meminit nostri?

Terraene caelo perfrueris memor,
qualem insiti divinitus ingeni
   dotes in angustis foventem
      pauperies tulit arta pagi :

qui vincit obstans immerito genus,
praetervolanti se citus applicat
   Fortunae et adversis repugnat
      sideris impatiens iniqui :

vim donec instans protulit igneam,
et clave tandem praeditus aurea
   stat Roma quid decernat auctor,
      quo patribus sonet ore Caesar :

And moving up from high to higher,
　　Becomes on Fortune's crowning slope
　　The pillar of a people's hope,
The centre of a world's desire;

Yet feels as in a pensive dream,
　　When all his active powers are still,
　　A distant dearness in the hill,
A secret sweetness in the stream,

The limit of his narrower fate,
　　While yet beside its vocal springs
　　He play'd at counsellors and kings,
With one that was his earliest mate;

Who ploughs with toil his native lea,
　　And reaps the labour of his hands,
　　Or in the furrow musing stands;
'Does my old friend remember me?'

TENNYSON.

mox arce rerum semper in altius
tendens resistit, publica civium
  tutela, quem sperans in uno
    sollicitus veneratur orbis.

idem remissis est ubi viribus
collem quieta deses imagine
  requirit Arpinum, requirit
    dulcis adhuc saliceta rivi,

angustiorum limitis artium,
donec canoris accola fontibus
  reges senatoresque primi
    cum socio simulabat aevi:

qui sulcat aegre rus patrium, metens
quos sevit agros, aut patitur boves
  cessare, dum secum: meine
    forte vetus meminit sodalis?

TIMON.

YET thanks I must you con,

That you are thieves profess'd, that you work not

In holier shapes: for there is boundless theft

In limited professions. Rascal thieves,

Here's gold. Go, suck the subtle blood o' the grape,

Till the high fever seethe your blood to froth,

And so 'scape hanging; trust not the physician;

His antidotes are poison, and he slays

More than you rob; take wealth and lives together;

Do villany, do, since you protest to do't,

ΤΙΜΩΝ.

δεῖ μήν τιν᾽ ἀλλὰ τοῦδέ μ᾽ εἰδέναι χάριν,
οἳ γ᾽ ἐκ προδήλου κλέπτετ᾽ οὐδὲ τἀσεβεῖν
ὡς εὐσεβεῖς ἀσκεῖτε· ταῖς γὰρ ἐννόμοις
τεχνῶν ἕπονται μυριοπληθεῖς κλοπαί.
ὅδ᾽, ὦ πανοῦργοι, χρυσός· ἔρρετ᾽, ἀμπέλου
αἷμ᾽ ὀξὺ κάρτ᾽ ἐκπίνεθ᾽, ὥστ᾽ ἀκμῇ φλογὸς
ζέοντα πέλανον ἐξαφρίζεσθαι φλεβῶν,
ᾅδου κρεμαστοῦ φεῦξιν· ἰατρῷ δ᾽ ὅπως
πείσεσθε μηδέν· ὀλοὰ γὰρ τὰ φάρμακα,
κτείνει δὲ πλείους κεῖνος ἢ συλᾷ κλοπεύς.
οὐχ οὓς ἀποστερεῖτε κἀξολεῖθ᾽ ἅπαξ,
μηδ᾽ ἣν ἐπαγγέλλεσθε χειρωναξίαν

4—2

Like workmen.   I'll example you with thievery:

The sun's a thief, and with his great attraction

Robs the vast sea: the moon's an arrant thief,

And her pale fire she snatches from the sun:

The sea's a thief, whose liquid surge resolves

The moon into salt tears: the earth's a thief,

That feeds and breeds by a composture stolen

From general excrement; each thing's a thief;

The laws, your curb and whip, in their rough power

Have uncheck'd theft.

SHAKESPEARE.

χρήσεσθ᾽ ἀτέχνῳ; καὶ τὰ συγκλέπτοντ᾽ ἐρῶ·
κλοπεὺς ὁ Φοῖβος, ὅς γ᾽ ἄλ᾽ ἄσπετον πολὺς
ἕλκων μαραίνει· ταὐτὸ δ᾽ οὐκ ὀφλισκάνει
Φοίβου σελήνη χλωρὸν ἁρπάζουσα φῶς;
κλέπτει δὲ πόντος ἁλμυρὸν μήνης δάκρυ
τήκων ὑγρῷ κλύδωνι· τῷ δὲ δρῶσ᾽ ἴσον
γῆ παντόφυρτον κλέμμα παγκοίνου σκατὸς
κυεῖ ῥοφοῦσα· κοὐδὲν ἔσθ᾽ ὁποῖον οὐ
κλέπτει χαλινὸς αὐτίχ᾽ οἱ νόμοι κλοπῆς
μάστιξ τ᾽ ἔχουσ᾽ ἄπειρον αὐθαδεῖς κλοπήν.

Tears, idle tears.

TEARS, idle tears, I know not what they mean,
Tears from the depth of some divine despair
Rise in the heart, and gather to the eyes,
In looking on the happy Autumn-fields,
And thinking of the days that are no more.

Fresh as the first beam glittering on a sail,
That brings our friends up from the underworld,
Sad as the last which reddens over one
That sinks with all we love below the verge;
So sad, so fresh, the days that are no more.

Desiderium.

O lacrimae, lacrimae, quo numine miror, inanes,
nescio quid lacrimae plusquam mortale sequentes
ingenti desiderio, nascuntur in imo
corde, rigant oculos, simul aurea messibus arva
conspicor et lapsos revoco sub pectore soles.

   quale novom velo iubar albescente renidet,
devexis cui forte sui redduntur ab austris;
quale iubar maestis supremum navis inaurat
carbasa, dimidium vitae abscondentis in aequor;
tam veteri manet albus honor, tam lugubris aevo.

Ah, sad and strange as in dark summer dawns

The earliest pipe of half-awaken'd birds

To dying ears, when unto dying eyes

The casement slowly grows a glimmering square;

So sad, so strange, the days that are no more.

TENNYSON.

ac veluti dubiis sub lucem aestate tenebris

fit vigilum male nidorum vagitus ; at aegro

auscultat sensu moriens, cui lumina cernunt

sublustrem iam stare magis magis aegra fenestram ;

tam lapsi subit aegra die, tam tristis imago.

STANZAS.

In a drear-nighted December,
Too happy, happy tree,
Thy branches ne'er remember
Their green felicity;
The north cannot undo them,
With a sleety whistle through them,
Nor frozen thawings glue them
From budding at the prime.

In a drear-nighted December,
Too happy, happy brook,
Thy bubblings ne'er remember,
Apollo's summer-look;

CARMEN.

Horreant, arbos, tenebrae Decembris;
at, quater fausto Iove, te vietam
nulla fortunae speciosioris
          cura remordet.
sibilans tutis aquilo minatur
grandinem ramis: male pertinaci
stringit amplexu glacialis umor
          vere novandos.

rive, contristet fera bruma noctes;
tu tamen, dulci nimis use fato,
immemor spumas calido decori
          sidere Phoebi:

But with a sweet forgetting
They stay their crystal fretting,
Never, never petting
About the frozen time.

Ah! would 'twere so with many
A gentle girl and boy!
But were there ever any
Writhed not at passéd joy?
To know the change and feel it,
When there is none to heal it,
Nor numbéd sense to steal it—
Was never said in rhyme.

KEATS.

tu remulcentis patiens veterni
vitrea parcis trepidare lympha,
nescius pigrae vicis insolenter
      ferre catenam.

virgines o si iuvenesque nuper
fervidi Lethen biberent eandem!
sed quis angori moderetur orbus
      deliciarum?
'unde quo veni?' dolor ingementis,
nulla quem vincit medicina, nullus
decipit torpor, quibus exprimatur
      carmina quaerit.

DARKNESS.

I had a dream, which was not all a dream.
The bright sun was extinguished, and the stars
Did wander darkling in the eternal space,
Rayless and pathless, and the icy earth
Swung blind and blackening in the moonless air;
Morn came and went—and came, and brought no day.

     *   *   *   *   *   *   *

The rivers, lakes and ocean all stood still,
And nothing stirred within their silent depths;
Ships sailorless lay rotting on the sea,

ΣΚΟΤΟΣ.

ὄνειρον εἶδον ᾧ τι κἀκ θεοῦ προσῆν·
φλὸξ ἡλίου γὰρ ἔφθιτ᾽, ἐπλανᾶτο δὲ
σκότον δεδορκότ᾽ ἄστρα πρωτάρχῳ χάει
ἀμαύρ᾽, ἀβουκόλητα· γῆ δ᾽ ἐπάλλετο
κρυσταλλοπὴξ κατ᾽ αἰθέρ᾽ οὐ μήνης ὕπο
τυφλή, κελαινωθεῖσα· φωσφόρος δ᾽ ἕως
διεξόδοισιν οὐ ξυνείπεθ᾽ ἡμερῶν.
ηὗδον δὲ λίμναι, ῥεῖθρά θ᾽ ηὗδ᾽, ηὗδεν Θέτις,
ἦν δ᾽ οὐδὲν ἀψόφοισιν ἔμψυχον βυθοῖς·
νῆες δ᾽ ἐσήποντ᾽, ὥστ᾽ ἀποιμάντου σκάφους

And their masts fell down piece-meal: as they dropp'd
They slept on the abyss without a surge—
The waves were dead: the tides were in their grave,
The moon, their mistress, had expired before;
The winds were wither'd in the stagnant air,
And the clouds perish'd! Darkness had no need
Of aid from them—She was the Universe.

LORD BYRON.

σαθρὸν καταρρεῖν ἱστόν, ὃς καταρρυεὶς
αὐτοῦ θαλάσσῃ νηνέμῳ κοιμίζεται.
οὐκ ἦν κλυδὼν ἔτ', οὐ παλιρροία σάλου,
μήνῃ θανούσῃ ξυνθανοῦσα κυρίᾳ·
ἔβριζε δ' αἰθὴρ πᾶσαν αὐάνας πνοήν,
φροῦδαί τε νεφελαί· συμμάχων γὰρ οὐκ ἔδει
τούτων τυραννεύοντα τοῦ παντὸς σκότον.

J. T.   5

Many a year is in its grave.

MANY a year is in its grave
Since I cross'd this restless wave ;
And the evening, fair as ever,
Shines on ruin, rock and river.

Then in this same boat beside,
Sat two comrades, old and tried ;
One, with all a father's truth ;
One, with all the fire of youth.

Umbrae.

Plurima iam periit volvendis mensibus aestas
    mobilis ut nostram transtulit unda ratem:
nec iuga nunc alia tingit dulcedine vesper,
    cana situ tingit moenia, tingit aquas.
tum geminos notaeque fide veterisque sodales
    non aliud mecum cymba ferebat iter:
alter in officiis constans mihi paene paternis;
    ut iuvenes fervent, fervidus alter erat.

5—2

One on earth in silence wrought,
And his grave in silence sought:
But the younger, brighter form
Passed in battle and in storm.

So, whene'er I turn my eye
Back upon the days gone by,
Saddening thoughts of friends come o'er me,—
Friends who closed their course before me.

Yet what binds us friend to friend
But that soul with soul can blend?
Soul-like were those hours of yore—
Let us walk in soul once more!

Take, O boatman, thrice thy fee—
Take, I give it willingly;
For, invisible to thee,
Spirits twain have crossed with me.

LONGFELLOW.

alterius tacitos exhausit vita labores,

 exhaustum tacita morte reliquit opus :

sed puer ille ferox et ovans volitare per ora

 martis ab horrisonis fugit in astra minis.

sic lapsi quoties sub corde remetior aevi

 tempora praeteritos respicioque dies,

tristis amicorum viduo succurrit imago,

 quis prior obvenit quam mihi meta viae.

quid tamen est aliud quod amico nectat amicum

 quam quod mente potest mens propiore frui ?

viximus ut vivont exutae corpora mentes :

 mentibus hic etiam quid vetat ire pares ?

ivimus—at triplex tu, portitor, accipe naulum,

 accipe non segni dona repensa manu :

scilicet una lacum transibat et altera mecum,

 sic tamen ut visus falleret umbra tuos.

BRUTUS.

It must be by his death: and for my part,

I know no personal cause to spurn at him,

But for the general. He would be crown'd:

How that might change his nature, there's the question.

It is the bright day that brings forth the adder;

And that craves wary walking. Crown him?—that;—

And then, I grant, we put a sting in him,

That at his will he may do danger with.

The abuse of greatness is, when it disjoins

ΒΡΟΥΤΟΣ.

φονᾷ τὸ πρᾶγμα· κᾆτ᾽ ἔμοιγ᾽ ἀνὴρ δοκεῖ
κόλασμα λακπάτητον οὐκ ὀφλισκάνειν,
εἰ μή τι τοῖς πλείστοισι. κοιρανεῖν ἐρᾷ·
μέλλων τί πάσχειν; τοῦτο δὴ ζητητέον.
πρόσειλος ἦ γ᾽ ἔχιδνά τοι φαντάζεται,
ἵν᾽ εὐλαβεῖσθαι τοῖς ὁδοιπόροις ἀκμή.
καὶ δὴ τύραννος γέγονε· χαιρέτω πόλις·
κέντρον γὰρ εἴη τῷδ᾽ ἄν, οὐκέτ᾽ ἀντερῶ,
ἐνθεῖσ᾽ ὅτῳ δύναιτ᾽ ἂν οὓς θέλοι δάκνειν.
διαφθορὰ γὰρ ἥδε τῆς ἀρχῆς ἔφυ
ἐν ᾧ τὸν οἶκτον τοῦ κράτους ἐχώρισεν·

Remorse from power : and, to speak truth of Cæsar,
I have not known when his affections sway'd
More than his reason.   But 'tis a common proof,
That lowliness is young ambition's ladder,
Whereto the climber upward turns his face :
But when he once attains the upmost round,
He then unto the ladder turns his back,
Looks in the clouds, scorning the base degrees
By which he did ascend.   So Cæsar may ;
Then, lest he may, prevent.

SHAKESPEARE.

ἐκμαρτυρήσω δ᾽ οὐκ ἰδὼν τῷ Καίσαρι
γνώμης ποτ᾽ αἰδῶ κρεῖσσον᾽ ἴσχουσαν ῥοπήν.
καίτοι θάμ᾽ ἦν ἔνδηλος ἡ ταπεινότης
κλῖμάξ τις οὖσ᾽ ἄρχοντι μειζόνων ἐρᾶν,
πρὸς ἥν τις ἐστήριξεν ἀμβάτης κάρα·
ἄκρον δὲ βαθμὸν οὐ φθάνει κατασχεθὼν
καὶ νωτίσας τὴν κλίμακ᾽ εἶτ᾽ ἀπεστράφη,
μετάρσιόν τ᾽ ἔβλεψεν, αἷς ἐπήκρισεν
ἐξωριάζων δουλίους προσαμβάσεις.
ἃ κἂν ποιῆσαι Καῖσαρ· ἀλλ᾽ εἴργειν τὸ μή.

The Genius of the Wood.

I.

O'ER the smooth enamell'd green,
Where no print of foot hath been,
  Follow me, as I sing
  And touch the warbled string:
Under the shady roof
Of branching elm, star-proof,
  Follow me:
I will bring you where she sits
Clad in splendour as befits
  Her deity:
Such a rural queen
All Arcadia hath not seen.

SILVANUS.

Qua gemmis nitet integrum
   gramen, nec viridi pes nocuit solo,
mecum pergite, dum meis
   subtiles modulor carminibus fides,
ulmos sub patulas, nemus
   astrorum radiis impenetrabile.
ducam qua solium tenet
   dignis illa suo numine vestibus
splendens: nec dea rusticos
   hac unquam tenuit pulcrior Arcadas.

II.

Nymphs and shepherds, dance no more
  By sandy Ladon's lilied banks,
On old Lycæus or Cyllene hoar
  Trip no more in twilight ranks:
Though Erymanth your loss deplore
  A better soil shall give ye thanks.
From the stony Mænalus
Bring your flocks and live with us:
Here ye shall have greater grace
To serve the lady of this place;
Though Syrinx your Pan's mistress were,
Yet Syrinx well might wait on her:
  Such a rural queen
  All Arcadia hath not seen.

MILTON.

vos, nymphae et pecorum duces,
   neu Lado choreas nectere gaudeat
praetexens vada liliis,
   neu Pani videant sacra cacumina
Cylleneve diutius
   incertum trepidos ad iubar ordines.
vos arces Erymanthiae
   plorent, dum melior det plaga gratiam.
vestras Maenaleis procul
   saxis his pecudes addite pascuis :
hic nostri nemoris dea
   cultorum veniet lenior agmini.
ut vestro placeat deo
   Syrinx, iure tamen pareat huic erae
Syrinx : nec dea rusticos
   hac unquam tenuit pulcrior Arcadas.

Ode.

I.

THE merchant, to conceal his treasure,
　　Conveys it in a borrow'd name,
Euphelia serves to grace my measure,
　　But Cloe is my real flame.

II.

My softest verse, my darling lyre
　　Upon Euphelia's toilet lay,
When Cloe noted her desire
　　That I should sing, that I should play.

Ad Chloen.

Ut proprias ficto qui mittunt nomine merces
  dumque opibus metuont infitiantur opes,
sic in amore Chloes Glycerae mentimur amorem :
  haec speciem confert versibus, illa facem.
nugor apud Glyceram : mecum lyra cessat ibidem,
  apta satis domini questibus, apta dolis :
versiculos idem attuleram non melle carentes :
  forte rogat, nectam verba modosque, Chloe.

III.

My lyre I tune, my voice I raise,
  And with my numbers mix my sighs ;
And whilst I sing Euphelia's praise,
  I fix my soul on Cloe's eyes.

IV.

Fair Cloe blush'd : Euphelia frown'd :
  I sung and gazed ; I play'd and trembled :
And Venus to the Loves around
  Remark'd how ill we all dissembled.

                                        PRIOR.

nec mora, praeludo fidibus, cantare paratus :

    spirat amor, spirat mixtus amore timor.

ast ita de Glycera quod bellum est cumque loquebar

    ut colerem voltu plura loquente Chloen.

nec color huic unus nec frons innubila laesae :

    ipse queror, stupeo, blandior, uror, amo.

at Venus irridens dum multa iocantur Amores,

    istud ut infabre dissimulatur! ait.

J. T.

ASIA.

HE gave men speech, and speech created thought,
Which is the measure of the universe;
And Science struck the thrones of earth and heaven,
Which shook, but fell not; and the harmonious mind
Pour'd itself forth in all-prophetic song:
And music lifted up the listening spirit
Until it walk'd, exempt from mortal care,
Godlike, o'er the clear billows of sweet sound;
And human hands first mimick'd and then mocked,
With moulded limbs more lovely than its own,

ΑΣΙΑ.

φθογγὴν βροτοῖς ἔδωκε κἀκ φθογγῆς πάλιν
ἔβλαστε τοῦ ξύμπαντος ἓν μέτρον λόγος·
Σοφία δ᾽ ἔπηλυς γῆς τε καὶ θεῶν θρόνους
ἔσεισεν οὐ σφαλέντας· εὔρυθμος δὲ φρὴν
ἐπέδραμ᾽ ὕμνων ἀναβολὰς χρηστηρίους,
μελῳδίαισιν ὥστ᾽ ἀναπτερούμενον
θνητῶν τιν᾽ ἔξω ξυμφορῶν θεοῦ δίκην
βαίνειν ἐφ᾽ ὑγροῖς κύμασιν τερπνοῦ μέλους.
καὶ δὴ τελευτῶν εἶδος ἔσκωψεν βροτῶν
ὃ τοῦθ᾽ ὑπερβαίνουσαν ἐκ μιμουμένης

The human form, till marble grew divine,

And mothers, gazing, drank the love men see

Reflected in their race, behold, and perish.

He told the hidden power of herbs and springs,

And Disease drank and slept.   Death grew like Sleep.

He taught the implicated orbits woven

Of the wide-wandering stars ; and how the sun

Changes his lair, and by what secret spell

The pale moon is transform'd, when her broad eye

Gazes not on the interlunar sea,

He taught to rule, as life directs the limbs,

The tempest-wingèd chariots of the ocean,

And the Celt knew the Indian.   Cities then

Were built, and through their snow-white columns flow'd

The warm winds, and the azure æther shone,

And the blue sea and shadowy hills were seen.

Such, the alleviations of his state,

Prometheus gave to man ; for which he hangs

Withering in destin'd pain.

SHELLEY.

μορφὴν διαρθρῶν ἰσοθέοις τυκίσμασιν,
ὧν κάλλος αἱ γυναῖκες ἐνθυμούμεναι
ἔτικτον ἃς τίς οὐκ ἰδὼν ἁλίσκεται;
ἔδειξε δ' αὐτοῖς τἀκ φυτῶν κρηνῶν τ' ἄκη,
αἱρεῖ δὲ τοὺς πίνοντας ἐξ ἄλγους ὕπνος,
ὕπνου δὲ θάνατος ἐξομοιοῦται τρόποις.
πολυπλάνων δ' ἔφραζε συμπεπλεγμένας
ἄστρων κελεύθους στροφάδας, ἥλιόν θ', ὅθεν
τίν' ἔρχεται κευθμῶνα, καὶ μήνης κύκλον,
ποίαις ἐπῳδαῖς ὠχριᾷ κηλούμενος
πελάγους ἀναυγήτοισιν ἐν μεταλλαγαῖς.
λινόπτερ' οὖν ὀχήματ' ἐμψύχοις ἴσα
τίς ἄλλος ἐξηγήσατ' οἰακοστροφεῖν;
ἔγνω δὲ Κέλτης Ἰνδον.   εἶτα πλινθυφῆ
ἦν σταθμά, λευκὴν δ' εὐαεῖς παραστάδα
διῇσσον αὖραι, κυάνεος δ' ὤφθη πόλος
πόντου τε γλαυκὸν κῦμ' ὑπόσκιοί τ' ἄκραι.
τοιαῦτ' ἀφέρτου δαίμονος κουφίσματα
βροτοῖς Προμηθεὺς ηὗρεν, ὧν μετάρσιος
ταῖς μοιροκράντοις πημοναῖς αὐαίνεται.

On an Early Death.

A PEARLY dew-drop see some flower adorn
And grace with tender beam the rising morn;
But soon the sun permits a fiercer ray,
And the fair fabric rushes to decay.
Lo, in the dust the beauteous ruin lies;
And the pure vapour seeks its native skies.
A fate like this to thee, sweet boy, was given—
To sparkle, bloom and be exhaled to heaven.

LORD BYRON.

Elegia.

Nonne vides, luci quo pulcrior adsit origo,
    roscidus ut violae suave renidet honos?
mox simul indulget nimio sol fervidus igni
    candida festinat veris alumna mori.
sternitur, a, media quam non inhonesta ruina!
    halitus in caelum fragrat abitque suum.
par tibi sors, miserande puer: sic gratia fulsit,
    mellea sic animae redditur aura Iovi.

Ode.

Awake, Aeolian Lyre, awake!

　And give to rapture all thy trembling strings;

　From Helicon's harmonious springs

A thousand rills their mazy progress take:

The laughing flowers that round them blow

Drink life and fragrance as they flow.

Now the rich stream of music winds along

Deep, majestic, smooth and strong,

Through verdant vales and Ceres' golden reign:

Ad barbiton.

Accende cantus, barbite, Lesbios,
praesentioris conscia numinis
   accende sopitos calores :
      mille fluont Heliconis orti
puro scatentis carmine fontibus
rivi vagantes, daedala quos humus
   praetexit errantum renidens
      ducere nectareos odores.
nunc, leve marmor, Pierium melos
alto quietum flumine labitur
   valles per umbrosas et agros
      auricomae Cereri subactos :

Now rolling down the steep amain

Headlong, impetuous, see it pour;

The rocks and nodding groves rebellow to the roar.

O sovereign of the willing soul,

    Parent of sweet and solemn-breathing airs,

    Enchanting Shell! the sullen Cares

And frantic Passions hear thy soft control.

On Thracia's hills the Lord of War

Has curb'd the fury of his car,

And dropt his thirsty lance at thy command:

Perching on the sceptred hand

Of Jove, thy magic lulls the feather'd king

With ruffled plumes and flagging wing:

Quenched in dark clouds of slumber lie

The terror of his beak and lightnings of his eye.

GRAY.

nunc a iugorum culmine proruens
insanienti gurgitis impetu
    defertur : immugit ruina
      rupibus et nemori corusco.
o grata menti, non humilis sciens,
regina, cantus, tu potes igneos
    lenire, testudo, furores,
      difficilem potes, alma, curam :
quin et iubenti Threicius tibi
frenat volantes Armipotens equos
    hastamque ponit gestientem
      purpureos agitare rivos :
regi volucrum tu Iovis in manu,
dum torpet ala languidus horrida,
    blandire, trux rostrum soporis
      nube premens oculique fulmen.

PRINCE ARTHUR.   HUBERT.

A.   HAVE you the heart?   When your head did but ache,
      I knit my handkerchief about your brows,
      (The best I had, a princess wrought it me,)
      And I did never ask it you again:
      And with my hand at midnight held your head;
      And, like the watchful minutes to the hour,
      Still and anon cheered up the heavy time;
      Saying, What lack you? and, Where lies your grief?

ΑΡΤΟΥΡΟΣ. ΟΥΒΕΡΤΟΣ.

A. τλαίης δὲ πῶς ἄν; σοὶ γὰρ εὖτ᾽ ἤλγει κάρα,
   ζώνην κόμαισι σαῖς ἐπιζεύξας ἐμήν,
   ἐμῶν γ᾽ ἀρίστην, βασιλίδος δ᾽ ἔργον χερός,
   εἶτ᾽ οὐκ ἀπῄτουν· καὶ τὸ σὸν χεροῖν ἐμαῖν
   κάρα μεσούσης εὐφρόνης ἐβάστασα·
   γνώμων γὰρ ἕρπονθ᾽ ὡς βάδην τηρεῖ χρόνον
   ἐγερτὶ πικρὰν ὧδ᾽ ἐκούφιζον τριβήν,
   λέγων, τί χρῄζεις; πῇ δὲ τἄλγος ἱζάνει;

Or, What good love may I perform for you?

Many a poor man's son would have lain still

And ne'er have spoke a loving word to you;

But you at your sick service had a prince.

Nay, you may think my love was crafty love,

And call it cunning; do, an if you will:

If heaven be pleased that you must use me ill,

Why then you must.—Will you put out mine eyes?

These eyes that never did nor never shall

So much as frown on you?

H.   I have sworn to do it,

And with hot irons must I burn them out.

SHAKESPEARE.

ποίας δὲ δεῖ σε φιλτάτης ὑπουργίας;
φαύλου μὲν εἰσὶ πατρὸς οἷς βρίζειν παρὸν
οὐκ ἠξίωσάν σ' οὐδ' ἂν εὖ προσεννέπειν·
σοὶ δ' αὖ νοσοῦντι πρόσπολος παρῆν ἄναξ.
ἀλλ' οὐ φιλοῦντα δῆθεν εὐπρεπὴς λόγος
προσήκασεν φιλοῦντι· φάσκ', εἴ σοι χάρις·
εἰ δ' οὖν μολεῖν σε τοῦδε λυμαντήριον
θεοῖς δέδοκται, τοὔργον ἔστ' ἐργαστέον.
τλήσει σὺ τῶνδέ μ' ὀμμάτων τητώμενον,
τῶν οὔτε πρόσθεν οὐδ' ἐπισχόντων γε σοὶ
σκύθρωπον ὄψιν οὔτ' ἐφεξόντων ποτέ;

'ΟΥ. ἐνώμοτος γάρ εἰμι ποιήσειν τάδε·
ἀκμαῖς δὲ χρή σοι μ' ἐμπύροις φθείρειν κόρας.

To a Lady's Girdle.

THAT which her slender waist confined
Shall now my joyful temples bind :
No monarch but would give his crown
His arms might do what this has done.

It was my heaven's extremest sphere
The pale which held that lovely deer :
My joy, my grief, my hope, my love
Did all within this circle move.

A narrow compass! And yet there
Dwelt all that's good and all that's fair ;
Give me but what this riband bound—
Take all the rest the sun goes round.

WALLER.

Ad zonam.

Zona, solet gracilem qua cingere Lesbia formam,
    quam bene temporibus fit diadema meis!
Mygdonia vellet Croesus dicione pacisci,
    huic quod erat, Croeso munus ut esset idem.
haec mihi formosam saepsit custodia cervam,
    saepsit inaccessus quicquid Olympus habet.
spes ubi plena metus, ubi versaretur amandi
    dulcis amarities, sat dabat una loci.
zona quod haec vinxit proprio concede fruamur;
    sic tibi quod passim Phoebus oberrat habe.

J. T.

Iphigenia.

But she, with sick and scornful look averse,
   To her full height her stately stature draws;
" My youth," she said, " was blasted with a curse :
   " This woman was the cause.

" I was cut off from hope in that sad place
   " Which yet to name my spirit loathes and fears;
" My father held his hand upon his face;
   " I, blinded with my tears,

Iphigenia.

Tristis ad haec odiis voltuque aversa superbo

altior assurgens spectanda regia forma

illa refert: nostram scelus exitiale iuventam

abrupit: stetit haec caussae. de virginis aevo

transactum semel est: refugit crudelia castra

nunc etiam meminisse animus litusque nefandum.

astabat pater et dextra velaverat ora:

ipsa laborantes fletu gliscente susurros

7—2

" Still strove to speak : my voice was thick with sighs,
   " As in a dream.   Dimly I could descry
" The stern black-bearded kings with wolfish eyes
   " Waiting to see me die.

" The high masts flickered as they lay afloat,
   " The crowds, the temples waver'd, and the shore ;
" The bright death quivered at the victim's throat ;
   " Touch'd ; and I knew no more."

                                        TENNYSON.

nitor ut expediam : sed creber anhelitus illos
turbat, ut aegra trahens singultit murmura somnus.
vix torvi apparent reges, vix effera cerno
lumina, barbatam cerno expectare coronam
dum moriar. celsi procul in statione coruscant
ante oculos mali, iam coetus inhorruit undans,
iam curvos fluitat sinus et trepidante vacillant
templa iugo, sacrae fulgor iam letifer instat
cervici tetigitque semel sensumque peremit.

ARCITES.

ME thy pupil,
Youngest follower of thy drum, instruct this day
With military skill, that to thy laud
I may advance my streamer, and by thee
Be styled the lord o' day! Give me, great Mars,
Some token of thy pleasure!

> [*There is heard clanging of armour, with
> thunder, as the burst of a battle: they all
> rise and bow to the altar.*]

O great corrector of enormous times,

ΑΡΚΙΤΗΣ.   ΧΟΡΟΣ.

A.   σὺ δή με σοῦ μαθόντα σάλπιγγος δὲ σῆς
      ὀπαδὸν ἀνδρόπαιδα σήμερον δορὸς
      ἔργ' ἐκδιδάσκων δὸς τὸ σόν τ' αὔξειν κλέος
      πρόσω τε χωρήσαντα σημείων χλιδῇ
      σοῦ καλλίνικον εὖγμ' ἀνειπόντος λαβεῖν.
      ἴθ', ὦ μέγιστε, δεῖξον εὖ φρονῶν, Ἄρες.

ΧΟ. ἔφριξεν αἰθήρ· προσκυνῶμεν, ὦ φίλοι.

A.   μηνιμάτων ἄλαστορ οὐκ ἀνασχετῶν,

Shaker of o'er-rank states, thou grand decider

Of dusty and old titles, that heal'st with blood

The earth when it is sick, and cur'st the world

O' the plurisy of people: I do take

Thy signs auspiciously, and in thy name

To my design march boldly.—Let us go.

BEAUMONT AND FLETCHER.

πόλεις ὁ σείων τὰς ἄγαν ὠγκωμένας,

χρόνῳ μυδωσῶν παγκρατὲς τιμῶν βραβεῦ,

τομαῖς τομῶσαν γῆς ὁ κουφίζων νόσον,

ὁ σώμασιν σφριγῶσαν ἰσχναίνων χθόνα,

ἐδεξάμην τὸν ὄρνιν, ἐντολῇ δὲ σῇ

ἐς πεῖραν εἶμ' ἄτρεστος· ἀλλ' ὁρμώμεθα.

The Praise of Virtue.

THE sturdy rock, for all his strength,
  By raging seas is rent in twain;
The marble rock is pearsed at length
  With little drops of drizzling rain;
The oxe doth yield unto the yoke,
  The steele obeyeth the hammer's stroke;
The stately stagge that seems so stoute
  By yelping hounds at bay is set;

Laus Virtutis.

Sensit furentis saevitiam freti
arx nesciarum cedere rupium :
   nituntur immortale marmor
      exiguae terebrare guttae :
collo iuvencus fert docili iugum,
incude mucro fingitur, obstitit
   urgente latratu Laconum
      fisa suae modo cerva formae.

The swiftest bird that flies about

  Is caught at length in fowler's net;

The greatest fish in deepest brooke

  Is soon deceived by subtle hooke;

Yea, man himself, unto whose will

  All things are bounden to obey,

For all his wit and worthie skill,

  Doth fall at last and fade away.

There is no thing but time doeth waste;

  The heavens, the earth consume at last.

But Vertue sits triumphing still

  Upon her throne of glorious fame:

Though spiteful death must body kill,

  Yet hurts he not his vertuous fame,

But life or death, whatso betides

  The state of Vertue never slides.

MARSHALL.

praecellat ala, serius ocius
auceps volucrem retibus implicat :
　　rex ipse rivorum doloso
　　　　decipitur cito piscis hamo.
quin et potentes nos animantium,
tot nos honesti dotibus ingeni
　　artis tot insignes, caduci
　　　　labimur effluimusque saeclo.
nil est quod annis non pereat : perit
tellus, peribunt sidera : siderum
　　triumphat et terrae superstes
　　　　fulta sedens adamante Virtus,
secura leti gentibus invidi,
intaminatis integra laudibus,
　　immota, seu nudantur enses
　　　　seu quatiunt Acheronta manes.

DOROTHEA.

Thou fool!
That gloriest in having power to ravish
A trifle from me I am weary of:
What is this life to me? not worth a thought;
Or, if it be esteemed, 'tis that I lose it
To win a better: even thy malice serves
To me but as a ladder to mount up
To such a height of happiness, where I shall
Look down with scorn on thee and on the world;

ΔΩΡΟΘΕΑ.

ὦ μῶρ᾽, ὃς αὐχεῖς εἴ μ᾽ ἀφαρπάζειν σθένεις
φαῦλόν τι, φαῦλον κτῆμα δύσφορόν θ᾽ ἅμα·
τοῦ ζῆν ἐμοὶ τί κέρδος; οὐδαμοῦ λέγω·
πλὴν ἐς τοσοῦτον, εἰ μεταλλάξω βίον
τοῦ νῦν ἀμείνω· σὴ μὲν οὖν λώβη μόνον
ἐπακρισάσῃ, βαθμὸς ὥς, ὑπηρετεῖ
ὑψίθρονον πρὸς ὄλβον, οὗ καθημένη
καταφρονήσω σοῦ τε καὶ θνητῶν δύης·

Where, circled with true pleasures, placed above
The reach of death or time, 'twill be my glory
To think at what an easy price I bought it :
There's a perpetual spring, perpetual youth ;
No joint-benumbing cold, or scorching heat,
Famine, nor age, have any being there.

MASSINGER.

οὐ χαρμοναῖσι γνησίαις κυκλουμένη,
ἀειθαλής, ἄφθαρτος, εὐφρανθήσομαι
οἷ᾽ ἐκτίνοντες ἡλίκ᾽ ἀντειλήφαμεν.
ἥβη γὰρ ἔνθ᾽ ἄπαυστος ἄφθιτόν τ᾽ ἔαρ·
οὐκ ἀρθροκηδὲς ψῦχος, οὐ λάβρον σέλας,
οὐ λιμὸς οὐδὲ γῆρας οὐδέν ἐστ᾽ ἐκεῖ.

MYCERINUS.

So spake he, half in anger, half in scorn:
And one loud cry of grief and of amaze
Broke from his sorrowing people: so he spake;
And turning, left them there; and with brief pause,
Girt with a throng of revellers, bent his way
To the cool region of the groves he loved.
There by the river-banks he wandered on,
From palm-grove on to palm-grove, happy trees,

MYCERINUS.

Dixerat, iratus pariter pariterque superbus :
quem lamentantum excepit vox una suorum,
una indignantum. nec plura locutus in uno
destitit obtutu haerentes, nec multa moratus
lascivo stipante choro vestigia flexit
in nemus umbriferum placitaque sub arbore frigus.
  illic ad ripas fluvii in palmeta meabat
addita palmetis, silvae felicis in umbras

Their smooth tops shining sunwards, and beneath
Burying their unsunned stems in grass and flowers:
Where in one dream the feverish time of Youth
Might fade in slumber, and the feet of Joy
Might wander all day long and never tire:
Here came the king, holding high feast, at morn,
Rose-crowned; and ever, when the sun went down,
A hundred lamps beamed in the tranquil gloom,
From tree to tree, all through the twinkling grove
Revealing all the tumult of the feast,
While the deep-burnished foliage overhead
Splintered the silver arrows of the moon.

MATTHEW ARNOLD.

cuius leve nitent in solem culmina, at infra
sole caret gemmantem abdens se truncus in herbam.
possit ibi sopita semel ferventior aetas
fallere dum teritur : laetus velit error ibidem
ire dies totos neque delassetur eundo.

   huc epulas rite instaurans rex flore rosarum
mane nitens aderat crines ; hic semper amoenas
centum elucebant Phoebo vergente per umbras
perpetuis lychni ramis, quibus omne micabat
huc illuc nemus et festis laeta orgia mensis :
at ferrugineo rutilantes desuper auro
lunae intercipiunt frondes argentea tela.

Diaphenia.

DIAPHENIA like the daffadowndilly,
White as the sun, fair as the lily,
Heigh ho, how I do love thee!
I do love thee as my lambs
Are belovéd of their dams;
How blest were I if thou would'st prove me.

Diaphenia like the spreading roses,
That in thy sweet all sweets encloses,
Fair sweet, how I do love thee!
I do love thee as each flower
Loves the sun's life-giving power;
For dead, thy breath to life might move me.

In Lydiam.

Albae par violae, magis
 puro sole, magis candida liliis,
eheu, Lydia, qui meum
 pertentans animum fervet amor tui!
hoc te quo subolem gregis
 matres lacteolam pectore prosequor :
quis felicior audiat,
 tu spectare fidem si properes meam ?
o laetae similis rosae,
 o quaecunque vigent unica continens
in te suavia, quam places
 semper pulcra mihi, semper amabilis !
flores ut teneri iubar
 almum solis amant, sic ego Lydiam :
lucis scilicet exuli
 aspirans animam tu mihi suscites.

Diaphenia like to all things blesséd,

If all thy praises were expresséd,

Dear joy, how I do love thee!

As the birds do love the spring,

As the bees their careful king;

Then in requite, sweet virgin, love me!

Constable.

o dicenda quod uspiam
   fausti, tot veneres si foret eloqui,
omnes o mihi gaudium
   praeter delicias, gratior enites
quam ver est avibus novom,
   quam prudens populis, Lydia, rex apum.
cessas, quin face mutua
   mollescens referas, lux mea, gratiam?

THE KING OF DENMARK.

O, MY offence is rank, it smells to heaven,

It hath the primal eldest curse upon it,

A brother's murder!—Pray can I not,

Though inclination be as sharp as will;

My stronger guilt defeats my strong intent;

And, like a man to double business bound,

I stand in pause where I shall first begin,

And both neglect.   What if this curséd hand

ΒΑΣΙΛΕΥΣ.

οἴμοι, μίασμ' ἔχθιστον, οὐρανοῦ μύσος,
τοὐμὸν τόδ' ἀμπλάκημα, πρωτάρχου δ' ἀρᾶς
κληροῦχον, αὐτάδελφος αὐθέντης φόνος·
καὶ προστροπαῖς μὲν οὐδ' ἐὰν τεθηγμένη
φρὴν συνθέλῃ τὸ δόξαν ἐγκεῖσθαι σθένω·
σπεύδοντα γὰρ τὸ κρεῖσσον ἀντισπᾷ κακόν·
ὁρμὰς δὲ δισσὰς εἶς ὁποῖ' ὡρμημένος
πότερον προτίσω χρῆμ' ἀμηχανῶν λόγῳ
οὐδέτερον ἔργοις ἐκφέρω. καὶ δὴ φόνῳ

Were thicker than itself with brother's blood?

Is there not rain enough in the sweet heavens

To wash it white as snow?   Whereto serves mercy

But to confront the visage of offence?

And what's in prayer, but this twofold force,

To be forestallèd ere we come to fall,

Or pardoned, being down?   Then I'll look up;

My fault is past.   But O, what form of prayer

Can serve my turn?   Forgive me my foul murder!

That cannot be; since I am still possessed

Of those effects for which I did the murder,

My crown, mine own ambition, and my queen.

SHAKESPEARE.

πανώλεθρος χεὶρ ἥδε διπλάσιον πάχος
πέπηγ᾽ ὁμαίμῳ· χερνίβων διόσδοτον
οὐ ῥεῦμα παγκαίνιστον ὥστε κἂν ἴσην
χιόνι καθαίρειν; ἢ θεῶν τί βούλεται
οἶκτος μὲν εἰ μὴ σφάλματ᾽ ἀντιπρῷρ᾽ ὁρᾶν,
τί δ᾽ ἄλλο κέρδος πλὴν τόδ᾽ ἐν λιταῖς διπλοῦν,
τὸ μὲν φθάνειν σώζοντας ἄπταιστον θεούς,
τὸ δ᾽ αὖ νέμειν πταίσαντι σύγγνοιαν βροτῷ;
πρὸς ταῦτά τοι κατηφὲς ὀρθώσω βλέπος
ὡς ἐκπεφευγώς. εἶτ᾽ ἐγὼ ποίας λέγων
εὐχὰς τύχοιμ᾽ ἄν; τῷ παλαμναίῳ, θεοί,
συγγνῶτε· πῶς γάρ, κτήμαθ᾽ ὅς γ᾽ ἔθ᾽ ὧντινων
ἕκατι κἀφόνευσα τοὺς θρόνους τ᾽ ἔχω
καὶ τὴν δάμαρτα καὶ τὸ φιλότιμον ξυνόν;

THE LAST MAN.

ALL worldly shapes shall melt in gloom
  The Sun himself must die,
Before this mortal shall assume
  Its Immortality!
I saw a vision in my sleep,
That gave my spirit strength to sweep
  Adown the gulf of Time!
I saw the last of human mould,
That shall Creation's death behold,
  As Adam saw her prime!

MORTALIUM SUPERSTES.

Fas daedalae telluris imagines,
ipsum tenebris fas Hyperiona
   marcere : sic demum caduci
      sidereum iubar induemus.
vidi sub altis nocte soporibus
volvenda fassum tempora somnium,
   quo raptus annorum per aequor
      mente feror trepidante vates.
vidi, quot auras terricolae bibent,
unum peremptis stare superstitem,
   cui funus ostendetur orbis,
      ut nova luxuries Adamo.

The Sun's eye had a sickly glare,

   The Earth with age was wan,

The skeletons of nations were

   Around that lonely man !

Some had expired in fight,—the brands

Still rusted in their bony hands ;

   In plague and famine some !

Earth's cities had no sound nor tread ;

And ships were drifting with the dead

   To shores where all was dumb !

Yet prophet-like that lone one stood

   With dauntless words and high,

That shook the sere leaves from the wood

   As if a storm passed by,

Saying, We are twins in death, proud Sun,

Thy face is cold, thy race is run,

languebat oris sol male luridus,

tellus anili pallida taedio :

   stat gentis humanae superstes

      quem populi posuere circum

ossa interempti : marte sub hostico

hos scabra in albis spicula dexteris

   testantur occisos, necarat

      hos famis, hos mora lenta morbi.

stratis viarum non sonitus pedum,

non murmur ardet praetereuntium :

   torpente torpentes in oras

      remigio vaga fertur alnus.

stabat severi prodigus auguri,

stabat superbis impavidus minis,

   frondesque ut autumnalis auster

      flavicomo quatit aesculeto

vox gloriantis, Par venit exitus

utrique nostrum : te quoque frigora,

   Sol magne, te fatalis urget

      terminus et miseranda divis

'Tis Mercy bids thee go :

For thou ten thousand thousand years

Hast seen the tide of human tears,

    That shall no longer flow.

CAMPBELL.

sors aegra terrae. sat veteris mali,

sat lacrimarum saecula saeculis

nectens tuebaris : dolorum

ille semel requievit aestus.

From 'Enoch Arden.'

ALL these he saw; but what he fain had seen
He could not see, the kindly human face,
Nor ever hear a kindly voice, but heard
The myriad shriek of wheeling ocean-fowl,
The league-long roller thundering on the reef,
The moving whisper of huge trees that branch'd
And blossom'd in the zenith, or the sweep
Of some precipitous rivulet to the wave,

Naufragus.

Haec videt : illud abest quod maxima cura videndi,
voltus abest humanus, abest humana loquella,
non videt haec, non audit, at audiit innumerorum
stridere mergorum torquentia saecula gyros,
audiit ex alto glomerantum pondus aquarum
saxa fragore quati, vel in aethere murmura summo
bracchia motantis silvae, motantis honores
aerios, vel praecipitem prono agmine rivom

As down the shore he ranged, or all day long
Sat often in the seaward gazing gorge,
A shipwreck'd sailor, waiting for a sail:
No sail from day to day, but every day
The sunrise broken into scarlet shafts
Among the palms and ferns and precipices;
The blaze upon the waters to the east;
The blaze upon the island overhead;
The blaze upon the waters to the west;
Then the great stars that globed themselves in Heaven,
The hollower-bellowing ocean, and again
The scarlet shafts of sunrise, but no sail.

                                    TENNYSON.

in mare devolvi; sive errat solus ad undas
seu pelagus spectante diem sub caute fatigans
naufragus expectat navem: lux trudere lucem,
nulla venire rates, sed solibus addere soles
per palmas frangenda rubentis tela diei,
per iuga, per filices: furit ignibus aequor eois,
terra furit mediis, furit excedentibus aequor,
mox orbes magni astrorum grandescere caelo,
mox gravius mugire salum, mox rursus oborti
tela rubere die—nullum, nullum undique velum.

SATAN.

WHAT though the field be lost?
    All is not lost; the unconquerable will,
    And study of revenge, immortal hate,
    And courage never to submit or yield,
    And what else is not to be overcome :—
    That glory never shall his wrath or might
    Extort from me.   To bow and sue for grace
    With suppliant knee, and deify his power

ΣΑΤΑΝΑΣ.

τί δ' εἰ κυροῦμεν τῆς μάχης γ' ἐσφαλμένοι;
οὐ καὶ τὰ πάντ' ἐσφάλμεθ'· οὐ τὸ καρτερεῖν,
οὐ τὰς ἀσάντους καὶ μεταδρόμους ἀράς,
οὐ τὸν καμεῖσθαι μήθ' ὑποπτήξειν ποτὲ
μέλλοντα θυμὸν ἄλλο τ' εἴ τι δύσμαχον,
ταῦτ' οὔτ' ἀπειλῶν κεῖνος οὔτε μὴ βίᾳ
ἔμ' ἐξέλῃ ποτ'· ἀλλὰ προσπεσόνθ' ἕδρας
θακεῖν γονυπετεῖς ἐξισοῦν τε δαίμονι

Who from the terror of this arm so late
Doubted his empire; that were low indeed,
That were an ignominy and shame beneath
This downfall; since, by fate, the strength of gods,
And this empyreal substance, cannot fail:
Since, through experience of this great event,
In arms not worse, in foresight much advanced,
We may with more successful hope resolve
To wage by force or guile eternal war,
Irreconcileable to our grand foe,
Who now triumphs, and in the excess of joy
Sole reigning holds the tyranny of heaven.

MILTON.

τὸν ἄρτι παπτήναντα μὴ τυραννίδος
πρὸς τοῦδ᾽ ἁμάρτοι· παντὸς αἴσχιον τόδε
καὶ πτωμάτων ἂν οἷα νῦν πεπτώκαμεν
ἔχθιον εἴη πταῖσμα· τοιαύτην θεῶν
ἰσχύν τε σῶμά τ᾽ ἐκ πυρὸς κεκραμένον
φθίνειν πέπρωται μήποτ᾽· εἰδότες δ᾽ ἂν αὖ
οἷον τόδ᾽ ἠγωνίσμεθ᾽, ἐς δορὸς κρίσιν
χείρους μὲν οὔ, κρείσσους δὲ πρὸς προμηθίαν,
μετ᾽ ἐλπίδος μέλλοιμεν εὐτυχεστέρας
ἢ χερσὶν ἢ δόλοισιν ἀσπόνδῳ στάσει
ἐλᾶν ἀπαύστως τὸν μέγα στυγούμενον,
ὃς νῦν μεγαυχὴς περιχαρεῖ φρονήματι
ἔχει μόναρχος εἷς θεῶν τυραννίδα.

THE PROGRESS OF POESY.

YOUTH rambles on life's arid mount,
　　And strikes the rock, and finds the vein
And brings the water from the fount,
　　The fount which shall not flow again.

The man mature with labour chops
　　For the bright stream a channel grand,
And sees not that the sacred drops
　　Ran off and vanished out of hand.

AETATES POETAE.

Ire libet iuveni deserta per ardua vitae ;
  fausta manus rupem percutit, unda salit :
prolicit arcanum iuvenis de fonte liquorem,
  unde nihil posthac prolicietur aquae.
ille viro labor est, opus exercere ligonis,
  alveus ut pateat cui data lympha micet.
nescit enim tenues divino e flumine guttas,
  cum semel exierint, deperiisse semel.

And then the old man totters nigh
And feebly rakes among the stones,
The mount is mute, the channel dry,
And down he lays his weary bones.

MATTHEW ARNOLD.

mox loca nota senex gressu titubante revisens

saxa quid umoris, quaerit, adusta tegant.

a, scatebrae siluere iugo, caret alveus unda,

nec mora quin duro procubet ipse solo.

THE COMING OF ARTHUR.

And the fringe
Of that great breaker, sweeping up the strand,
Lash'd at the wizard as he spake the word,
And all at once all round him rose in fire,
So that the child and he were clothed in fire.
And presently thereafter follow'd calm,
Free sky and stars: "And this same child," he said,
"Is he who reigns; nor could I part in peace

ΑΡΤΟΥΡΟΣ ΕΠΙΦΑΙΝΟΜΕΝΟΣ.

ἀκτῇ δ᾽ ἐπενθοροῦσα ταῦτ᾽ εἰρηκότα
ἔθεινεν ἄκρα μάντιν ἡ τρικυμία,
πύρπνους τ᾽ ἐπιζέσασα πᾶσ᾽ ἀνήλατο
ὥστ᾽ ἀμπέχεσθαι παῖδ᾽ ὁμοῦ καὐτὸν πυρί.
κᾆτ᾽ ἦν γαλήνη, καθαρά τ᾽ ἐξεφαίνετο
καθαρᾶς δι᾽ αἴθρας ἄστρ᾽· ὁ δ᾽, ἔσθ᾽ ὅδ᾽, εἶφ᾽, ὁ παῖς
ἀρχῆς ὁ νῦν κληροῦχος· οὐ γὰρ ἦν θέμις
ἐκπνεῖν ἐκήλῳ τοῖσδ᾽ ἐπ᾽ ἀρρήτοις ἐμοί.

J. T.

10

Till this were told." And saying this the seer
Went thro' the strait and dreadful pass of death,
Not ever to be question'd any more
Save on the further side; but when I met
Merlin, and ask'd him if these things were truth—
The shining dragon and the naked child
Descending in the glory of the seas—
He laugh'd as is his wont, and answer'd me
In riddling triplets of old time, and said:

"Rain, rain, and sun! a rainbow on the lea!
And truth is this to me, and that to thee;
And truth or clothed or naked let it be.

Rain, sun, and rain! and the free blossom blows;
Sun, rain, and sun! and where is he who knows?
From the great deep to the great deep he goes."

TENNYSON.

τοσαῦτα λέξας δυσπέρατον ἐκπερᾷ
στενωπὸν Ἀιδου μάντις, οὐ περαιτέρω,
οὐδ᾽ εἴ τις ἐξέροιτο, πλὴν ἐκεῖ, φράσων.
ἐγὼ δὲ τῷ Κάλχαντι συντυχοῦσ᾽ ὅτε
εἰ ταῦτ᾽ ἐτήτυμ᾽ εἴτε πλάστ᾽ ἀνηρόμην,
κέλσαι θαλάσσης παμφαοῦς περιστεφὲς
γυμνὸν δράκοντι ξὺν παναιόλῳ βρέφος,
γελῶν τὸ δὴ ξύνηθες ἀντεφθέγξατο
αἰνιγματωδεῖς καὶ παλαιφάτους στίχας·
  τῇδε μὲν αὐγῶν τῇδε δ᾽ ἀπ᾽ ὄμβρων
  κέχυται πολύχρους Ἶρις ἐπ᾽ ἀγροῖς·
  ἔστι δ᾽ ἀληθὲς τοῦτο μὲν ἡμῖν,
  ὑμῖν δ᾽ ἕτερον· σαφὲς οὖν ἔστω,
    κεκαλυμμένον εἴτ᾽ ἀκάλυπτον.
  ἡδὺ μὲν ὄμβροις ἡδὺ δ᾽ ἐν εἴλῃ
  καλύκων ἀνθεῖ γάνος αὐτοφυές·
  τίς δὲ διέγνω δνοφέρ᾽ εἰλικρινῶν
  βροτός; ἐξ ἀφανοῦς προφανέντ᾽ ἀφανὴς
    κευθμῶνος ἐδέξατο κευθμών.

ALTHÆA.

But thou, son, be not filled with evil dreams
Nor with desire of these things; for with time
Blind love burns out; but if one feed it full
Till some discolouring stain dyes all his life,
He shall keep nothing praiseworthy, nor die
The sweet wise death of old men honourable,
Who have lived out all the length of all their years
Blameless, and seen well-pleased the face of gods,
And without shame and without fear have wrought
Things memorable, and while their days held out
In sight of all men and the sun's great light

ΑΛΘΑΙΑ.

ὦ παῖ, σὺ δ᾽ αἰσχρῶν μήτ᾽ ὀνειράτων γέμε
μήθ᾽ ἱμέρου τοιῶνδε· καρτεροῦντι γὰρ
μαραίνεται τὸ μάργον· ᾧ δ᾽ ἂν ἐκτραφὲν
κηλῖδ᾽ ἄπαντος θῇ μελαμπαγῆ βίου,
τὰ χρήσθ᾽ ὅδ᾽ οὐ σώσαιτ᾽ ἄν, οὐκ εὐθνήσιμος
σοφῆς τελευτήσειεν ἐξ εὐγηρίας,
ἀναμπλάκητον καὶ τριτόσπονδον βίον
δίκην λαχόντων, οἳ κατ᾽ ὄμμα δαίμοσιν
ἐλθόντες εὐφράνθησαν, αἰσχύνης δ᾽ ἄτερ
ἤθλησαν οὐ τρέσαντες οὐκ ὀλούμενα,
αἰὼν δ᾽ ἕως ἀντεῖχεν οὐκ ἀμάρτυροι
πρὸς πάντ᾽ ἐποπτεύοντος ἡλίου φάος

Have gat them glory and given of their own praise
To the earth that bare them and the day that bred,
Home friends and far-off hospitalities,
And filled with gracious and memorial fame
Lands loved of summer or washed by violent seas,
Towns populous and many unfooted ways,
And alien lips, and native with their own.
But when white age and venerable death
Mow down the strength and life within their limbs,
Drain out the blood and darken their clear eyes,
Immortal honour is on them, having past
Through splendid life and death desirable
To the clear seat and remote throne of souls,
Lands undiscoverable in the unheard-of west,
Round which the strong stream of a sacred sea
Rolls without wind for ever, and the snow
There shows not her white wings and windy feet,
Nor thunder nor swift rain saith anything,
Nor the sun burns, but all things rest and thrive.

SWINBURNE.

δόξαν μὲν ἐκτήσαντο, τῆς δ' εὐδοξίας
θρέπτρ' ἀντέδωκαν παντρόφου τ' αὐγῇ θεοῦ
καὶ μητρὶ Γαίᾳ, χάρμα τοῖς πρὸς αἵματος
κήρυγμα δ' εὐξένοισι πολύφημον δόμοις·
καὶ τῶνδ' ἀείνως εὔχαρίς τ' ἔχει λόγος
θέρει ξυναύλους εἶθ' ἁλικλύστους πλάκας,
ἀγορῶν τε κύκλους ἀστιβεῖς τ' ἐρημίας
ἐγχωρίων τε στόματα κἀλλοθρῶν ἅμα.
λευκὸν δ' ἰδοῦσι γῆρας εἶθ' Ἅιδου σέβας
στέρνων παρηβήσασαν ἐξαμᾷ βίαν,
αἷμ' ἐξαμαυρῶν ὄμμα δ' ἀμβλωπὸν τιθείς,
γέρας τότ' ἔστ' ἄφθαρτον ἐξαφιγμένοις
κλεινὸν δι' αἰῶν' εὐφιλῆ τ' ἀπαλλαγὴν
μακάρων τιν' εἰς εὐῶπα τηλουρόν θ' ἕδραν,
ἀνευρέτους ἀγνῶτος Ἑσπέρου γύας,
οὓς δὴ θέορτος αἰὲν ἀμφελίσσεται
ἀνήνεμος πλημμυρίς, οὐδ' ἀελλόπους
λευκοπτέροις ῥιπαῖσιν ἔρχεται χιών,
οὐ σκηπτός, οὐκ ὀξεῖα δυσφημεῖ ψακάς,
οὐ καῦμ' ἔφλεξε, πάντα δ' εὐεστὼ τρέφει.

Her sufferings ended with the day.

Her sufferings ended with the day;
    Yet lived she at its close,
And breathed the long, long night away
    In statue-like repose.

But when the sun in all his state
    Illumed the eastern skies,
She passed through glory's morning gate
    And walked in Paradise.

                                JAMES ALDRICH.

Mora.

Iamque die non illa quidem vergente laborat,
    sed licet emeritam terra parumper habet ;
noctis enim tristes ultro remorata per horas
    linquere marmoreum noluit aura sinum.
at dubias splendens quom sol discusserat umbras,
    aurea quom toto lux oriente rubet,
digna triumphantem quae sic intraret Olympum
    asseritur superis mane Serena choris.

ROMEO.

O MY love! my wife!
Death, that hath suck'd the honey of thy breath,
Hath had no power yet upon thy beauty:
Thou art not conquer'd; beauty's ensign yet
Is crimson in thy lips and in thy cheeks,
And death's pale flag is not advanced there.
Tybalt, liest thou there in thy bloody sheet?
O, what more favour can I do to thee,
Than with that hand that cut thy youth in twain
To sunder his that was thine enemy?

ΡΩΜΕΩΝ.

ὦ φίλτατόν μοι νεογάμου νύμφης δέμας,
Ἀιδης ὃς ἐκπέπωκε σὸν πνοῆς μέλι
οὔπω προσωμίληκε τῇ γ᾽ εὐμορφίᾳ·
σὺ δ᾽ οὐχ ἑάλως, ἀλλ᾽ ἔθ᾽ ὡς παρῇδ᾽ ἔχων
χείλη τ᾽ ἐπαίρει σῆμα πορφυροῦς Ἔρως,
ὁ δ᾽ ὠχρὸς Ἀιδης οὐ τρόπαι᾽ ἔστησέ πω.
Τύβαλτε, σοῦ δ᾽ αὖ πτῶμα φοίνιον τόδε;
οἴμοι, τί δρῶν ἂν σοὶ χαριζοίμην πλέον
ἢ τὸν σὸν ᾗπερ συνταμὼν ἔχω βίον
ταύτῃ καθαιρῶν καὶ τὸν ἐνστάτην χερί;

Forgive me, cousin! Ah, dear Juliet,
Why art thou yet so fair? shall I believe
That unsubstantial death is amorous,
And that the lean abhorred monster keeps
Thee here in dark to be his paramour?
For fear of that, I still will stay with thee:
And never from this palace of dim night
Depart again: here, here will I remain
With worms that are thy chamber-maids; O, here
Will I set up my everlasting rest,
And shake the yoke of inauspicious stars
From this world-wearied flesh.

SHAKESPEARE.

συγγνῶθι, σύγγον'· ἀλλά, φιλτάτη, τί σοὶ
ἀκραιφνὲς ὧδε κάλλος; ἢ πεισθήσομαι
σκιάν περ Ἅιδην εἶτ' ἐρῶντα τυγχάνειν,
σὲ δ', ὄντ' ἄναιμον καὶ βροτοστυγῆ θεόν,
ὥς οἱ ξυνοικήσουσαν ἐν σκότῳ τρέφειν;
ὃ μὴ γένηται συμπαραστατεῖν δοκεῖ,
ἀποστατεῖν δὲ μηκέτ' ἐξ ἀνηλίων
νυκτὸς μελάθρων· ἐνθάδ', ἐνθάδ' ἐμμενῶ
εὐλαῖς τὸ λοιπὸν σαῖσι προσπόλοις ξυνών·
τούτων μέτοικος ἐγγραφεὶς αἰώνιος,
θνηταῖς ἀπειπὼν ξυμφοραῖσι, δαίμονος
δυσδαίμονος λέπαδνον ἐκτραχηλιῶ.

Witch-elms that counterchange the floor.

WITCH-ELMS that counterchange the floor
  Of this flat lawn with dusk and bright;
  And thou, with all thy breadth and height
Of foliage, towering sycamore;

How often, hither wandering down,
  My Arthur found your shadows fair,
  And shook to all the liberal air
The dust and din and steam of town:

Laelius.

O mixta fundens nigra clarioribus

in aequor, ulme, graminis,

o bracchiis superba diffluentibus,

sycomore, celso vertice :

quam saepe non invitus urbe Laelius

mutabat haec umbracula,

benigniori traditurus aetheri

lites, Suburam, fenora.

He brought an eye for all he saw;
   He mixt in all our simple sports;
   They pleased him, fresh from brawling courts
And dusty purlieus of the law.

O joy to him in this retreat,
   Immantled in ambrosial dark,
   To drink the cooler air, and mark
The landscape winking thro' the heat:

O sound to rout the brood of cares,
   The sweep of scythe in morning dew,
   The gust that round the garden flew,
And tumbled half the mellowing pears!

O bliss, when all in circle drawn
   About him, heart and ear were fed
   To hear him, as he lay and read
The Tuscan poets on the lawn:

nec venit arvis ipse non idoneus

    ludove dispar simplici,

raucis libenter actionibus vacans,

    Libone, Ianis, Marsya.

o quale tenebris otium fragrantibus

    reductioris anguli,

auraeque gratum frigus et nictantia

    vapore rura solstiti!

quo dissipentur ocius curae sono

    quam mane falcis impigrae,

vel quod piris hinc inde mitescentibus

    trahat ruinam, flaminis?

o quom beati cingeremus Laelium

    stratum in virenti caespite,

quam cordibus vox, quam placebat auribus

    vates legentis Atticos!

Or in the all-golden afternoon

A guest, or happy sister, sung,

Or here she brought the harp and flung

A ballad to the brightening moon.

TENNYSON.

vergente mox cantabat aureo die
  aut hospes aut Calpurnia,
vel illa sumpta iam nitescentem lyra
  admurmurabat Cynthiam.

DUKE.   VIOLA.

Vio.   Ay, but I know—

Duke.   What dost thou know?

Vio.   Too well what love women to men may owe:

In faith, they are as true of heart as we.

My father had a daughter loved a man,

As it might be, perhaps, were I a woman,

I should your lordship.

Duke.   And what's her history?

ΆΝΑΞ. ΌΥΙΟΛΗ.

ΟΥ. καίτοι σάφ᾽ οἶδα

Α.   πράγματος τίνος πέρι;

ΟΥ. λίαν τόδ᾽, οἷον ἀνδρὸς ἵμερον γυνὴ
τρέφειν πέφυκεν· ὡς ἐτητύμως δοκῶ
ἀνδρῶν γυναῖκας πίστιν οὐχ ἥσσω τελεῖν.
ἦν πατρὶ τὠμῷ παῖς τις, ἢ πόθῳ κέαρ
ἀνδρὸς κατέσχεθ᾽, ὥσπερ εἰ κἀγὼ γυνὴ
κυρῶν ἔρωτι σῷ κατασχοίμην, ἄναξ.

Α. τύχας ἂν ἤδη τῆσδ᾽ ἀναπτύσσοις κόρης.

Vio. A blank, my lord. She never told her love,

But let concealment, like a worm i' the bud,

Feed on her damask cheek : she pined in thought,

And with a green and yellow melancholy

She sat like patience on a monument,

Smiling at grief. Was not this love indeed?

We men may say more, swear more : but indeed

Our shows are more than will; for still we prove

Much in our vows, but little in our love.

SHAKESPEARE.

ΟΥ. κενήν γε δέλτον· οὐ γὰρ ἐξεῖπέν ποτε
ἔρωτα δηξίθυμον· ἡ σιγὴ δ' ἀεί,
λειχῆνος ἐν κάλυξιν ἠριναῖς δίκην,
χροιᾶς ἐβόσκετ' ἄνθος· ἐν δὲ φροντίσιν
ἐτήκετ'· ὠχρὰ δ' ἄλγεσιν μελαγχόλοις
κάθητο, τλήμων ὥς τις ἐν στήλῃ θεά,
γελῶσα λύπῃ· πῶς τάδ' οὐκ ἔργοις ἔρως;
λόγων μὲν ὅρκων θ' ἄνδρες ἀφθονώτεροι,
τῆς δ' εὐπρεπείας λείπεται προθυμία·
καὶ γὰρ λόγῳ μὲν πόλλ' ὑπισχνούμεσθ' ἀεί,
ἔρως δ' ἐπ' ἔργοις σμικρὸς ἐξελέγχεται.

ARTHUR.

YET think not that I come to urge thy crimes;

I did not come to curse thee, Guinevere,

I, whose vast pity almost makes me die

To see thee laying there thy golden head,

My pride in happier summers, at my feet.

The wrath which forced my thoughts on that fierce law,

The doom of treason and the flaming death,

(When first I learnt thee hidden here) is past.

ΑΡΤΟΥΡΟΣ.

μή νυν παρεῖναί μ᾽ ὡς κατήγορον δόκει·
ἥκω γὰρ οὐκ ἀραῖά σ᾽ αὐδήσων, γύναι,
μόνον μὲν οὖν, ὡς ᾤκτισ᾽, οὐ ψυχορραγῶν,
ἰδών σε θεῖσαν ὧδε χρυσανθὲς κάρα
θερῶν ἄγαλμα φιλτέρων χαμαιπετές.
ὀργὴ γὰρ ἥ μ᾽ ἐπ᾽ ὠμὸν ἦγ᾽ ὠμὴ νόμον
φέροντα τοῖς προδοῦσιν ἔμπυρον δίκην,
ὡς πρῶτον ἤδη σ᾽ οἳ πέφευγας, οἴχεται.

The pang—which while I weigh'd thy heart with one
Too wholly true to dream untruth in thee,
Made my tears burn—is also past, in part.
And all is past, the sin is sinn'd, and I,
Lo! I forgive thee, as Eternal God
Forgives: do thou for thine own soul the rest.
But how to take last leave of all I loved?
O golden hair, with which I used to play
Not knowing! O imperial moulded form,
And beauty such as never woman wore,
Until it came a kingdom's curse with thee—
I cannot touch thy lips, they are not mine,
But Lancelot's: nay, they never were the king's.

TENNYSON.

ἄλγος δ', ὃ τἀμὰ πρὸς τὸ σὸν σταθμωμένῳ
πίστ' ὄντα μᾶλλον ἢ σὲ μὴ πιστὴν νέμειν
κλαῦμ' ἦπτε θερμόν, καὶ τόδ' ἔσθ' ἵν' οἴχεται.
τί δ' οὐ παρῴχηκ'; εἴργασαί μ' οἷ' εἴργασαι·
κἀγώ, βροτοῖσιν ὥσπερ ἄφθιτος πατήρ,
ἰδού, ξυνέγνων· σὴν σὺ τἄλλ' ἀκοῦ φρένα.
χαίρειν δὲ πῶς δὴ τλῶ λέγειν τὰ φίλτατα;
ὦ χρυσοφεγγεῖς, παῖγμ' ἐμὸν χεροῖν, τρίχες,
ἤδη γὰρ οὐδέν· ὦ δέμας τυραννικόν,
ὦ κάλλος οἷον τίς ποτ' εἴληχεν γυνή,
ἔστ' ἠμπολήθη, σοὶ ξυνόν, λύμη πόλει·
χείλη τάδ' οὐ φιλοῖμ' ἂν οἷς Πάρις φίλος,
ἀνὴρ δ' ὅδ' οὐκέτ'· ἦν μὲν οὖν οὐπώποτε.

The Dead.

HE who hath bent him o'er the dead
Ere the first day of death is fled,
The first dark day of nothingness,
The last of danger and distress,
(Before Decay's effacing fingers
Have swept the lines where beauty lingers,)
And marked the mild angelic air,
The rapture of repose that's there,

Mortua.

Qualis inhaeret amans qui lumina clausit amatae,
 cum trahitur damno prima recente dies,
prima dies tenebrarum, orbati prima silenti,
 summa laborantis speque metuque precis,
ante resolvendae quam signa morantia formae
 tabida Persephones audet obire manus:
ora velut placidae cernit clementia divae
 non enarrandum pacis habere iubar;

The fix'd yet tender traits that streak
The languor of the placid cheek,
And—but for that sad shrouded eye,
   That fires not, wins not, weeps not now,
   And but for that chill, changeless brow,
Where cold obstruction's apathy
Appals the gazing mourner's heart,
As if to him it could impart
The doom he dreads, yet dwells upon ;
Yes, but for these and these alone,
Some moments, ay, one treacherous hour,
He still might doubt the tyrant's power ;
So fair, so calm, so softly seal'd,
The first, last look by death reveal'd !
Such is the aspect of this shore,
'Tis Greece, but living Greece no more !

LORD BYRON.

purpureae cernit vestigia mollia lucis

    tingere languentes, nec maculare, genas.

quin nisi quod maerens oculis obducitur umbra,

    qui face, qui fletu blanditiisque carent;

nescius humano nisi quod mollescere luctu

    ille rigor durae marmora frontis habet,

unde reformidans gelidae contagia mortis

    horret, et horrescens, quod timet, orbus amat;

cetera paulisper possitve beatus in horam

    credere Plutonis non domuisse minas:

tanta quies, tam dulce silens componit honestas

    quod suprema dies fertque rapitque decus.

non alius decor hac etiam spectatur in ora:

    Graecia, sed non iam Graecia viva, manes.

THE DREAM.

A CHANGE came o'er the spirit of my dream.
The Boy was sprung to manhood: in the wilds
Of fiery climes he made himself a home,
And his soul drank their sunbeams: he was girt
With strange and dusky aspects: he was not
Himself like what he had been; on the sea
And on the shore he was a wanderer;
There was a mass of many images

ʼΟΝΕΙΡΟΝ.

καῦθις τροπαίαν προσγελᾷ μ᾽ ὄναρ πνέον·
ὁ παῖς γὰρ ἐξήνδρωτο· γῆς δ᾽ ἀνημέρου
ἐπιστροφὰς κατεῖχεν ἡλιοστιβεῖς,
εὐῶπα δ᾽ ἐξέπινεν ἡλίου βίαν·
μέλας μὲν ἀμφεχεῖτο βάρβαρος λεώς,
ἔπασχε δ᾽ ἔσθ᾽ ὁ καὐτός· εἶχε δ᾽ οἰόφρων
θαλασσόπλαγκτον κἀπὶ ῥηγμῖνος πλάνην.
ἐνταῦθ᾽ ἐπιρρεῖ πυκνὰ μὲν πλημμυρίδος

Crowded like waves upon me, but he was
A part of all; and in the last he lay
Reposing from the noontide sultriness,
Couch'd among fallen columns, in the shade
Of ruin'd walls: where by his sleeping side
Stood camels grazing, and some goodly steeds
Were fastened near a fountain: and a man
Clad in a flowing garb did watch the while,
While many of his tribe slumbered around:
And they were canopied by the blue sky,
So cloudless, clear and purely beautiful,
That God alone was to be seen in Heaven.

LORD BYRON.

τρόποισι φάσμαθ', ᾧ δ' ἐκεῖνος οὐ προσῆν,
ὅσ' εἶδον, οὐδ' ἕν· καὶ τὰ μὲν παρῴχετο·
ὁ δ' ηὗδεν ἤδη πῦρ μεσημβρινὸν φυγών,
κλιθεὶς ἐν ἄγαις κιόνων, ἐρειπίοις
τοίχων σκιασθείς· οὗ παρεστάτουν λέχει
νομάδες κάμηλοι, καί τι πρὸς κρήνῃ τέλος
εὔπωλον ἦν σειραῖον· εἱμένος δέ τις
στολμοὺς ποδήρεις ἵσταθ' ἡμεροσκόπος,
ἐν φυλέταις ἄϋπνος εἷς κοιμωμένοις·
τοῖς δ' ἦν κατασκήνωμα λαμπρὸν αἰθέρος,
ἄχραντον, εὐπρόσωπον, εὐαγὲς γελῶν
ὥστ' ἄλλο μηδὲν πλὴν τὸ θεῖον ἐμπρέπειν.

HYMN

ON THE MORNING OF CHRIST'S NATIVITY.

It was the winter wild,
While the Heaven-born Child
    All meanly wrapped in the rude manger lies:
Nature in awe to Him
Had doffed her gaudy trim,
    With her great Master so to sympathize:
It was no season then for her
To wanton with the sun, her lusty paramour.

HYMNUS.

Stridebat auras sollicitans hiemps
quom sordido velamine rustici
    praesepis in cunis iacebat
        Patre Puer genitus supremo:
cui laetum amictus exuerat decus
Natura sorti morigerans Dei:
    non illa lascivo protervam
        igne frui sinit hora solis.

Only with speeches fair

She woos the gentle air

    To hide her guilty front with innocent snow,

And on her naked shame,

Pollute with sinful blame,

    The saintly veil of maiden white to throw,

Confounded, that her Maker's eyes

Should look so near upon her foul deformities.

But He, her fears to cease,

Sent down the meek-eyed Peace ;

    She, crowned with olive green, came softly sliding

Down through the turning sphere

His ready harbinger,

    With turtle wing the amorous clouds dividing,

And waving wide her myrtle wand,

She strikes an universal peace through sea and land.

tantum precatur lene sonantibus

obedientem vocibus aera,

   celetur incestata castis

      frons nivibus, tegat impudico

contaminatae flagitio scelus

candore vestis virgineo premens,

   ne labe pollutam nefanda

      Rex oculo propiore visat.

atqui timentem Caelipotens iubet

Pax lenis astans lumine mulceat;

   quae laeta delabens ab axe

      nuntia sidereo, revincta

crines olivae fronde, sequacia

ceu turtur ala nubila dividit,

   myrtoque vibrata quietum

      alma salum domat, alma terras.

No war or battle's sound

Was heard the world around :

    The idle spear and shield were high up hung ;

The hookéd chariot stood

Unstained with hostile blood ;

    The trumpet spake not to the arméd throng ;

And kings sat still with awful eye,

As if they surely knew their sovran Lord was by.

But peaceful was the night

Wherein the Prince of Light

    His reign of peace upon the earth began :

The winds with wonder whist

Smoothly the waters kissed,

    Whispering new joys to the mild ocean,

Who now hath quite forgot to rave,

While birds of calm sit brooding on the charméd wave.

non orbe toto martis erat sonus,

non conferentum signa cohortium :

  hastile defunctamque parmam

    militia paries habebat :

non falx cruorem traxerat hosticum,

non excitabant armigeros tubae :

  Regem fatebantur venire

    ora metu pavefacta regum.

nox ipsa puro consiluit polo

qua splendidorum Sceptriger ordinum

  decrevit immortale pacis

    imperium stabilire terris :

aurae stupentes oscula fluctibus

dantes quietis gaudia praecinunt,

  quos ala parcentes moveri

    alcyonum premit incubantum.

The stars with deep amaze

Stand fixed in stedfast gaze,

   Bending one way their precious influence,

And will not take their flight,

For all the morning light,

   Or Lucifer that often warned them thence;

But in their glimmering orbs did glow,

Until their Lord himself bespake, and bid them go.

And though the shady gloom,

Had given day her room,

   The sun himself withheld his wonted speed,

And hid his head for shame,

As his inferior flame

   The new enlightened world no more should need;

He saw a greater Sun appear

Than his bright throne, or burning axletree, could bear.

haerent in uno sidera desuper

intenta visu, dum pia numine

   unum superfuso coronant :

     nec reducis face pulsa lucis

cedunt monenti Lucifero fugae,

ignes micantum non prius orbium

   pressura quam tempus morandi

     Caelipotens vetet ipse duci.

quin, orta quanquam dispulerat dies

umbras nigrantes, ipse volantibus

   nolebat indulgere bigis

     sol faciem pudebundus abdens :

non his beatas senserat ignibus

egere terras, non tolerabilem

   sedi coruscanti rotisque

     flammiferis renitere Solem.

The shepherds on the lawn,

Or e'er the point of dawn,

    Sat simply chatting in a rustic row;

Full little thought they then,

That the mighty Pan

    Was kindly come to live with them below;

Perhaps their loves, or else their sheep,

Was all that did their silly thoughts so busy keep.

When such music sweet

Their hearts and ears did greet,

    As never was by mortal finger strook,

Divinely-warbled voice

Answering the stringéd noise,

    As all their souls in blissful rapture took:

The air, such pleasure loth to lose,

With thousand echoes still prolongs each heavenly close.

herba sedentes ordine rustico

simplex bubulci colloquium novae

   sub lucis adventum serebant:

     quos latuit, reor, otiosos

Pan magnus astris terricolum domos

mutare dignans. maior ovilium,

   fortasse maior distinebat

     cura leves animos amorum.

tum mentem et aures alliciunt soni

iucundiores quam quibus intremat

   terrestre plectrum; dum canoris

     caelicolum velut arte chordis

vox apta sensus commovet intimos,

cui mille lentus reddit imagines,

   ne maius humano repente

     intereat modulamen, aer.

Nature that heard such sound,

Beneath the hollow round

    Of Cynthia's seat, the airy region thrilling,

Now was almost won

To think her part was done,

    And that her reign had here its last fulfilling;

She knew such harmony alone

Could hold all heaven and earth in happier union.

At last surrounds their sight

A globe of circular light,

    That with long beams the shamefaced night arrayed;

The helméd cherubim,

And sworded seraphim,

    Are seen in glittering ranks with wings displayed,

Harping in loud and solemn quire,

With unexpressive notes to Heaven's new-born Heir.

quas ipsa voces aetheris in plagis

Natura lunae sub solio poli

  convexa pertentare mirans

    paene suo fore iam labori

regnoque finem credidit ultimum :

nec postulari iam sua foedera

  ut terra cum caelo iugetur,

    quos melius iuget ille cantus.

mox solis instar suspicientibus

affulget orbis flammifer immicans

  noctis verecundae tenebris :

    stant galea gladioque clari

Regis ministri caelitis alites,

dum rite pleno murmure carminum

  non eloquendorum Parentis

    exoriens celebratur Heres.

Such music (as 'tis said)

Before was never made,

 But when of old the sons of morning sung,

While the Creator great

His constellations set,

 And the well-balanced world on hinges hung,

And cast the dark foundations deep,

And bid the weltering waves their oozy channel keep.

Ring out, ye crystal spheres,

Once bless our human ears

 (If ye have power to touch our senses so),

And let your silver chime

Move in melodious time,

 And let the base of heaven's deep organ blow,

And with your ninefold harmony

Make up full consort to the angelic symphony.

cantasse solos huic parili lyra

nascente mundo caelicolas ferunt,

cum finxit Aeternus lacunar

sidereum, stabilivit orbis

iusto renixos pondere cardines,

rerum columnas inviolabiles

abstrusit, undantis subegit

claustra pati maris uda fluctus.

delectet aures o semel insonans

crystallinorum carminis orbium

quod fas sit exaudire nobis :

o numeros crepet in canoros

subtile plectrum, dum gravior tonat

immugientis spiritus aetheris,

vocesque caelestum sequatur

vox novies modulata caeli !

For if such holy song

Enwrap our fancy long,

Time will run back and fetch the age of gold,

And speckled Vanity

Will sicken soon and die,

And leprous Sin will melt from earthly mould,

And Hell itself will pass away,

And leave her dolorous mansions to the peering day.

Yea, Truth and Justice then

Will down return to men,

Orbed in a rainbow; and like glories wearing

Mercy will sit between,

Throned in celestial sheen,

With radiant feet the tissued clouds down steering,

And Heaven, as at some festival,

Will open wide the gates of her high palace hall.

nam sacra cordi musa diutius

si blandietur, tempus in aureum

   horae recurrent, iam libido

      tabe diem maculosa claudet,

noxae resolvet terricolas lues,

ipsum inferorum ius abolebitur,

   rimanda pandentur diei

      atria Tartarei doloris.

tum cincta crines iride Veritas

terris redibit Iustitiae comes;

   quas inter effulgens, sororum

      par decori decus ipsa gestans,

nubes coruscas mille coloribus

splendente findet tramite Lenitas,

   et feriabuntur reclusis

      templa poli spatiosa portis.

But wisest Fate says no,

This must not yet be so,

   The Babe lies yet in smiling infancy,

That on the bitter cross

Must redeem our loss

   So both Himself and us to glorify :

Yet first to those ychained in sleep

The wakeful trump of doom must thunder through the deep,

With such a horrid clang

As on Mount Sinai rang,

   While the red fire and smouldering clouds out brake :

The aged earth aghast,

With terror of that blast,

   Shall from the surface to the centre shake ;

When at the world's last session

The dreadful Judge in middle air shall spread His throne.

at Parca prudens hoc negat illico

sic exiturum. parvus adhuc Puer

subridet in cunis, acerba

in cruce terricolis piamen

laturus olim, qua sibi gloriam

nobisque quaerat: sed prius (audient

sopore devincti) profundum

fata ciens tuba personabit:

qualis minarum vox Sinaitidas

concussit arces quom rutilantibus

flammis et exundante fumo

ignivomae micuere nubes:

grandaeva miro territa classico

tellus medullis pertremet intimis,

quom sede Quaesitor supremum

gentibus aeria residet.

And then at last our bliss

Full and perfect is,

   But now begins; for, from this happy day,

The old dragon, underground

In straiter limits bound,

   Not half so far casts his usurpéd sway,

And, wroth to see his kingdom fail,

Swinges the scaly horror of his folded tail.

The oracles are dumb,

No voice or hideous hum

   Runs through the archéd roof in words deceiving.

Apollo from his shrine

Can no more divine,

   With hollow shriek the steep of Delphos leaving.

No nightly trance, or breathéd spell,

Inspires the pale-eyed priest from the prophetic cell.

tum plena demum gaudia nos manent,

nunc ordiuntur. primus enim dies

   hic claustra lucescit draconi

      Tartareo magis arcta passo,

iniuriarum dimidio minus

ius proferenti, dum solio fremit

   orbandus et quassat retorquens

      squamigerae fera flagra caudae.

oracla torpent : non laquear replent

horrenda vanis murmura vocibus :

   non ipse Delphorum futura

      praecinit ex adytis Apollo,

ferale, rupem dum fugit, eiulans :

non somnio, non carmine mystico

   pallentis obtutum ministri

      fatidicum penetrale turbat.

The lonely mountains o'er

And the resounding shore

 A voice of weeping heard and loud lament;

From haunted spring and dale

Edged with poplar pale

 The parting genius is with sighing sent;

With flower-inwoven tresses torn

The nymphs in twilight shade of tangled thickets mourn.

In consecrated earth

And on the holy hearth

 The Lars and Lemures moan with midnight plaint;

In urns and altars round

A drear and dying sound

 Affrights the Flamens at their service quaint;

And the chill marble seems to sweat,

While each peculiar power foregoes his wonted seat.

solis iugorum nenia, litori

immurmuranti flebilis insonat:

    iam carmen ad caeleste fontes

      iam solitas trepidare valles,

quas cana cingit populus, ingemens

Faunus relinquit, iam nemoris Dryas

    spissi per obscurum revinctas

      flore comas lacerata maeret.

ad busta noctu flent Lemures, gemit

intaminati Lar periens foci:

    urnis inhorrescens et aris

      lugubris et moriens querella

prisca exsequentes carmina flamines

terret, videntur frigida marmora

    sudare dum sedem relinquens

      quisque suam fugit incolarum.

Peor and Baälim

Forsake their temples dim,

   With that twice battered god of Palestine;

And moonéd Ashtaroth,

Heaven's queen and mother both,

   Now sits not girt with taper's holy shine;

The Lybic Hammon shrinks his horn,

In vain the Tyrian maids their wounded Thammuz mourn.

And sullen Moloch fled

Hath left in shadows dread

   His burning idol all of blackest hue;

In vain with cymbals' ring

They call the grisly king,

   In dismal dance about the furnace blue;

The brutish gods of Nile as fast,

Isis, and Orus, and the dog Anubis, haste.

delubra iam sublustria deserunt

Peorque Belusque et Syriae deus

   quem stravit haud simplex ruina :

     cornua iam Libycus retraxit

Ammon, iacentem iam Tyriae gemunt

Thaumanta frustra, nec genitrix deum

   et praeses Astarte Selenes

     cincta piis levat ora taedis.

formidolosis in tenebris atrox

linquens Moluchus fugit imaginem

   ignes per admotos nigrantem :

     nec chorus ut quatiat laborans

circa caminum cymbala luridum,

rex torvus audit. par rapit Isidem,

   par terror Horum, par Anubim,

     Niliacae sacra monstra ripae.

Nor is Osiris seen

In Memphian grove or green,

    Trampling the unshowered grass with lowings loud:

Nor can he be at rest

Within his sacred chest,

    Nought but profoundest hell can be his shroud;

In vain with timbrelled anthems dark

The sable-stoléd sorcerers bear his worshipped ark.

He feels from Juda's land

The dreaded Infant's hand,

    The rays of Bethlehem blind his dusky eyn;

Nor all the gods beside

Longer dare abide,

    Not Typhon huge ending in snaky twine:

Our Babe, to show His Godhead true,

Can in His swaddling bands control the damnéd crew.

iam non Osirim, dum nemoris vias,

dum prata passu proterit arida,

   miratur immugire Memphis :

     cista deum premit inquietum

imi premendum tegmine Tartari :

frustra, insonantes carmina tympanis

   horrenda, ferali vehentes

     veste magi venerantur arcam.

intendit Infans Iudaicis procul

surgens in oris attonito manum :

   visus laborantes oborti

     lux hebetat nova Bethlemitae :

nec ceteri iam di neque desinens

Typhon in orbes anguineos manet :

   testatur in cunis quis instet

     ausa regens Puer impiorum.

So when the sun in bed,

Curtained with cloudy red,

    Pillows his chin upon an orient wave,

The flocking shadows pale

Troop to the infernal jail,

    Each fettered ghost slips to his several grave,

And the yellow-skirted fays

Fly after the night-steeds, leaving their moon-loved maze.

But see the Virgin blest

Hath laid her Babe to rest,

    Time is our tedious song should here have ending.

Heaven's youngest-teeméd star

Hath fixed her polished car,

    Her sleeping Lord with handmaid lamp attending:

And all about the courtly stable

Bright-harnessed angels sit in order serviceable.

MILTON.

sic quom cubilis sol etiam latens

post vela rubris texta vaporibus

  os fulcit eois fretorum,

    Tartareus rapit agmen umbras

exsangue carcer : quaeque suum petunt

vinctae sepulcrum, nec croceae choros

  luna sub arridente nectunt

    noctis equos famulae sequentes.

ast ecce Natum composuit sinu

felice Virgo; iam numeros decet

  finire longos : ecce leves

    qua minima nitet aethra currus

iam stella iunxit, fax domini torum

ministra servans, dum stabulum tuens

  regale caelestum sub armis

    prompta cohors operae refulget.

ODE.

INTIMATIONS OF IMMORTALITY FROM RECOLLECTIONS OF EARLY CHILDHOOD.

I.

THERE was a time when meadow, grove, and stream,
The earth, and every common sight,
  To me did seem
  Apparelled in celestial light,
The glory and the freshness of a dream.
It is not now as it hath been of yore;
  Turn wheresoe'er I may,
   By night or day,
The things which I have seen I now can see no more.

ΑΝΑΜΝΗΣΙΣ.

ἦν χρόνος εὖτε νάπαι καὶ πίσεα καὶ ῥυτὸν ὕδωρ

καὶ χθονὸς ὅσσα τύχοιμι συνήθεά περ ποτιλεύσσων

φέγγος ἐφαίνετ' ἔμοιγε διόσδοτον ἀμφιέσασθαι,

θεσπεσίην ἀκτῖνα ποταίνιον ὥσπερ ὀνείρου·

ἀλλ' ἃ τότ' ἦν ἔστ' οὐκέτ'· ἐγὼ γὰρ ὅποι κε τράπωμαι

οὔθ' ὁρόω νύκτωρ τὰ πρὶν εἴσιδον οὔτε μετ' ἦμαρ.

II.

The Rainbow comes and goes,
And lovely is the Rose,
The Moon doth with delight
Look round her when the heavens are bare,
Waters on a starry night
Are beautiful and fair ;
The sunshine is a glorious birth ;
But yet I know, where'er I go,
That there hath past away a glory from the earth.

III.

Now while the birds thus sing a joyous song,
And while the young lambs bound
As to the tabor's sound,
To me alone there came a thought of grief :
A timely utterance gave that thought relief,
And I again am strong :
The cataracts blow their trumpets from the steep ;
No more shall grief of mine the season wrong ;
I hear the Echoes through the mountains throng,
The Winds come to me from the fields of sleep,

ἔρχεαι ὡς πάρος, Ἶρι, καὶ οἴχεαι· ἡδὺ δὲ λάμπει
ὄμμα ῥόδου, χαίρει δὲ περισκοπέουσα σελήνη
οὐρανὸν εὖτ᾽ ἀκάλυπτος ὑπερράγη ἄσπετος αἰθήρ·
ἱμερόεν δέ τι νυκτὸς ὑπαὶ πόλῳ ἀστερόεντι
νάματα μαρμαίρει, μάλα τ᾽ ἡλίου ἀγλαομειδὲς
ὀρνυμένοιο πρόσωπον· ἐγὼ δέ τοι οἷ κεν ἀλῶμαι
ἔσθ᾽ ὅ τι δὴ χθονὸς οἶδα παναίολον ἐξαπολωλός.

νῦν δ᾽, ὅτε πᾶς ὄρνις φιλόφρον μέλος ὧδε μελίζει,
εὖτ᾽ ἄρνες σκαίρουσι νεότροφοι οἷον ὑπ᾽ αὐλῶν,
μούνῳ ἐπῆλθεν ἔμοιγέ τι πένθιμον· ἀλλ᾽ ἐπικαίρως
ἐξειπὼν τόδ᾽ ἔλυσα καὶ ἔρρωσμαι πάλιν ἤδη.
σαλπίζουσι μὲν ὑψόθ᾽ ἀπ᾽ ἠλιβάτοιο φάραγγος
ῥηγνύμενοι χείμαρροι· ἐγὼ δέ τοι αἴσιον ὥρην
οὐκέτ᾽ ἄχει μιανῶ· διὰ γὰρ πτύχας ἀρθὲν ὀρεινὰς
Ἠχοῦς μυριόφωνον ἐπιρροθέει κελάδημα,
λειμώνων τέ μοι ὕπνου ἀποπνείουσιν ἀϋτμαί·

14—2

And all the earth is gay;
          Land and sea
Give themselves up to jollity,
          And with the heart of May
Doth every beast keep holiday;—
          Thou Child of Joy,
Shout round me, let me hear thy shouts, thou
          happy Shepherd-boy!

IV.

Ye blessed Creatures, I have heard the call
          Ye to each other make; I see
The heavens laugh with you in your jubilee;
          My heart is at your festival,
          My head hath its coronal,
The fulness of your bliss, I feel—I feel it all.
          Oh evil day! if I were sullen
          While Earth herself is adorning,
               This sweet May-morning,
          And the Children are culling
               On every side,
          In a thousand valleys far and wide,
          Fresh flowers; while the sun shines warm,
And the Babe leaps up on his Mother's arm:—

χθών τε γέγηθεν ἅπασα, φιλοφροσύνῃσί τ᾽ ἀνεῖται

πόντος ὁμοῦ καὶ γαῖα, θέρει τε σὺν ἠπιοθύμῳ

πάνθ᾽ ἅμ᾽ ἑορτάζοντα συνήδεται ἔθνεα θηρῶν·

Εὐφροσύνῃ φίλε κοῦρε, σὺ δ᾽ ἀμφί μοι αἶρε βοητύν,

οἰοπόλ᾽, ὡς ὀλόλυγμα τορῶς σέθεν, ὄλβι᾽, ἀκούω.

  ἔκλυον, οὔ με παρῆλθε, μακάρτατοι, οἷα θροεῖτε

ἀντίτυπ᾽ ἀλλήλοις, ἴδον ἀνθεστήρι᾽ ἀγόντων

αἰθέρ᾽ ὕπερθε γελῶντα, πάρειμι δὲ καὐτὸς ἑορτῇ

ὅσσον ὁμοφρονέειν γε, κόμας τ᾽ ἀνέδησα καὶ αὐτὸς

μυρί᾽ ἰαινόμενος μετὰ μυρί᾽ ἰαινομένοισιν.

ἦ μάλα κεν πέλοι ἦμαρ ἀναίσιον εἰ σκυθρὸς εἴην

νῦν ἐγὼ εὖτ᾽ ἠῶθι θέρους γλυκυμειλίχου ὥρῃ

γαῖα μὲν ἀγλαΐην περιβάλλεται, ἐν δὲ νάπῃσιν

ἄνθε᾽ ἀνηρίθμοισιν ἐερσήεντα δρέπονται

παῖδες ἑκάς τε πέλας τε, φίλον τ᾽ ἐπιδέδρομεν εἴλης

καῦμα, βρέφος τ᾽ ἀνάθρωσκει ἐν ἀγκαλίδεσσι τεκούσης·

I hear, I hear, with joy I hear!

—But there's a Tree, of many, one,

A single Field which I have looked upon,

Both of them speak of something that is gone:

The pansy at my feet

Doth the same tale repeat:

Whither is spread the visionary gleam?

Where is it now, the glory and the dream?

v.

Our birth is but a sleep and a forgetting:

The Soul that rises with us, our life's Star,

Hath had elsewhere its setting,

And cometh from afar:

Not in entire forgetfulness,

And not in utter nakedness,

But trailing clouds of glory do we come

From God, who is our home:

Heaven lies about us in our infancy!

ἦ τάδ᾽ ἀκήκο᾽, ἀκήκο᾽, ἐϋφράνθην δέ τ᾽ ἀκούων.

ἀλλὰ γὰρ ἐκ πολλῶν μεμέληκέ μοι ἕν γέ τι δένδρον

εἷς ἀγρός, ὥ τ᾽ ἄμφω μὲν ἐπέδρακον εἰσορόων δὲ

οἶδά τι καὶ ποθέων· τὸ δὲ πὰρ ποσὶ ταὐτὸν ὑπεῖπε

λευκόϊον· ποῖ δὴ φάσμ᾽ ἀγλαὸν ἐκπεπόταται;

ποῦ κ᾽ ἔτι μαρμαρόεντος ἰδοίμεθα φέγγος ὀνείρου;

   κῶμα μόνον λήθη τε βροτῶν γένος· ἦ δὲ σὺν ἡμῖν

ψυχὴ γιγνομένοισιν ἀνέσχεθε, μόρσιμος ἀστήρ,

ἄλλοθί που καταδῦσ᾽ ἕκαθέν ποθεν ἐξανέτειλεν.

οὐκ ἄρα δὴ πάντων γε λελασμένοι, οὐκ ἄρα γυμνοὶ

πάντη γ᾽, ἀλλ᾽ αἴγλην τιν᾽ ἐφελκόμενοι νεφελάων

δῶμα πατρὸς προλιπόντες ἱκάνομεν ἀθανάτοιο.

ἀμφὶ βρέφος νεαρὸν τέταται φάος οὐρανιώνων·

Shades of the prison-house begin to close
    Upon the growing Boy,
But he beholds the light, and whence it flows
    He sees it in his joy;
The Youth, who daily farther from the east
    Must travel, still is Nature's Priest,
    And by the vision splendid
    Is on his way attended:
At length the Man perceives it die away,
And fade into the light of common day.

VI.

Earth fills her lap with pleasures of her own:
Yearnings she hath in her own natural kind,
And even with something of a Mother's mind,
    And no unworthy aim,
    The homely Nurse doth all she can
To make her Foster-child, her Inmate Man,
    Forget the glories he hath known,
And that imperial palace whence he came.

παιδὶ δ᾽ ἐπ᾽ αὐξομένῳ στυγερὸν κνέφας ἆσσον ἐφέρπει,

εἱρκτῆς οἷα δεθεῖσιν· ὅμως δ᾽ ἐπίδερκτον ἐκείνῳ

φῶς τε μένει πηγαί τε φάους ταρφθέντι νοῆσαι·

ὃς δ᾽ ἄρ᾽ ἔφηβος ἐὼν φεύγει πλάκ᾽ ἐπ᾽ ἦμαρ ἑῴαν,

ἔστ᾽ ἔτι τῆς Φύσεως ἱερεὺς ὅδε, λαμπρὸν ἔθ᾽ ἕρπει

φάσμα πρόπομπον ἔχων· ὁ δ᾽ ἐν ἀνδράσιν εὖτε λέλεκται,

δὴ τότ᾽ ἀποφθιμένων ὕπαρ εἴσιδε φαῦλον ὀνείρων.

τερπνὰ μὲν ἐκ κόλπων, ὅσα γήϊνα, γαῖα προτείνει·

ἔστι γὰρ ὡς θνητῇ θνητῶν πόθος· ὡς δέ γε μήτηρ

κεδνὰ φρεσὶν νωμῶσα, τροφός περ ἄγροικος ἐοῦσα,

θρέμμ᾽ ἑὸν ἱμείρει, βροτὸν ὃν τ᾽ ἔχει ᾧ ἐνὶ οἴκῳ,

ἐκλελαθεῖν ὅσ᾽ ἀγαστὰ πάρος ποτ᾽ ἔχαιρε θεωρῶν

οἷά τε δώματ᾽ ἔλειπεν ἐπουρανίου βασιλῆος.

VII.

Behold the Child among his new-born blisses,

A six years' Darling of a pigmy size!

See, where 'mid work of his own hand he lies,

Fretted by sallies of his mother's kisses,

With light upon him from his father's eyes!

See, at his feet, some little plan or chart,

Some fragment from his dream of human life,

Shaped by himself with newly-learned art;

  A wedding or a festival,

  A mourning or a funeral,

   And this hath now his heart,

  And unto this he frames his song:

   Then will he fit his tongue

To dialogues of business, love, or strife;

  But it will not be long

  Ere this be thrown aside,

  And with new joy and pride

The little Actor cons another part;

ἠνίδε γὰρ νεαρὸν μετὰ χάρμασι παῖδα νεόρτοις,

ἑξαετές τι θάλος, τυτθὸν δέμας, ὄμμα δόμοιο·

ἠνίδε χειρὸς ἑῆς νιν ἐν ἔργμασι κείμενον, οἵοις

μητρὸς ἐπισσυμένοισι φιλήμασι πυκνὰ πέπασται,

ὡς γανόων οἱ πατρὸς ἐπιρρέει ἵμερος ὄσσων·

ἠνίδε δέλτιόν οἵ τι παραὶ ποσὶν ἠέ τι πλάσμα,

δεῖγμα βίου τόν τ’ αὐτὸς ὀνειροπολῶν ὑπέγραψεν,

ἀρτιδαεῖ τεύχων σοφίῃ γάμον ἤ τιν’ ἑορτὴν

εἴτε ταφῆς πένθημα· φιλεῖ γὰρ νῦν τάδε θυμῷ,

τῶνδε μέλος τεκταίνει ἐπίσκοπον· εἶτα νεμόντων

πράγματ’ ἐριζόντων τε λόγοις ὀάροισί τ’ ἐραστῶν

γλῶσσαν ἂν ἁρμόσσειε· χρόνος δ’ οὐ πολλὸς ἐπέσται

καὶ τάδε μὲν ῥίψει, καινῇ δέ κε τέρψεϊ γαίων

ἄλλο μαθὼν δρᾶμ’ αὖθις ἀγωνίζοιτο νεοσσός·

Filling from time to time his "humorous stage"
With all the Persons, down to palsied Age,
That Life brings with her in her equipage;
    As if his whole vocation
    Were endless imitation.

VIII.

Thou, whose exterior semblance doth belie
    Thy Soul's immensity;
Thou best Philosopher, who yet dost keep
Thy heritage, thou Eye among the blind,
That, deaf and silent, read'st the eternal deep,
Haunted for ever by the eternal mind,—
    Mighty prophet! Seer blest!
    On whom those truths do rest,
Which we are toiling all our lives to find,
In darkness lost, the darkness of the grave;
Thou, over whom thy Immortality
Broods like the Day, a Master o'er a Slave,
A presence which is not to be put by;

κωμῳδῶν δ᾽ ἐσάγει τὰ μὲν ἄρτι πρόσωπα, τὰ δ᾽ ἐξῆς,

παντοδάπ᾽, ἐν δὲ γέροντας ἐκωμῴδησε τελευτῶν

γυῖ᾽ ἀμενεῖς, ὅσσοισι βίος σὺν ὀπάοσι πομπὴν

πέμπει ἐφημερίων, ὡς οὐκ ἄρ᾽ ἐπ᾽ ἄλλο τι ταχθεὶς

πλὴν τόδε, μιμήσεις μιμήσεσιν ἔμπεδ᾽ ἀμείβειν.

ὦ βρέφος, οὗ δοκέει φαῦλον δέμας εἰσορόωντι,

ἀλλὰ σύνοικον ἔχει ψυχῆς μέγα κάρτος ἀπείρου·

ὦ πανάριστε σοφῶν, ὃς ἔτ᾽ οὐρανόθεν τά τ᾽ ἐδέξω

σῴζεαι, ἔν τε τυφλοῖσι βλέπων μόνος, οὔτε τι φωνῶν

οὔτε κλύων, δέρκει τελετὰς αἰῶνος ἀβύσσου,

ταῖς σε νόος μυέων αἰώνιος οὐκ ἀπολήγει·

μάντι μέγιστε, πάνολβε, καταστεφὲς οὐρανοδείκτων

οἷα διαὶ βίου ἄνδρες ἀμαυροὶ ψηλαφόωμεν

εἰν ὄρφνῃς πλαγχθέντες ἀναυγήτοις Ἀΐδαο·

σεῖο γὰρ ἀθάνατος δαίμων Ὑπερίονος αὐγαῖς

ἶσος ὑπερκρέμαται, βασιλεύς θ᾽ ὡς θῆτος ἀνάσσων

ἠνεκέως τε πάρεστι καὶ οὐκ ἐθέλει παρεῶσθαι·

Thou little Child, yet glorious in the might
Of heaven-born freedom on thy being's height,
Why with such earnest pains dost thou provoke
The years to bring the inevitable yoke,
Thus blindly with thy blessedness at strife?
Full soon thy Soul shall have her earthly freight,
And custom lie upon thee with a weight,
Heavy as frost, and deep almost as life!

IX.

O joy! that in our embers
Is something that doth live,
That nature yet remembers
What was so fugitive!
The thought of our past years in me doth breed
Perpetual benediction; not indeed
For that which is most worthy to be blest;
Delight and liberty, the simple creed
Of Childhood, whether busy or at rest,
With new-fledged hope still fluttering in his breast:—

παιδίον, ἰσχύϊ θάλλον ἐλευθερίης θεοφάντῳ

ζωῆς ἐν κορυφῇσι, τί δὴ χρόνον ὧδέ σ' ἀνάγκης

ἐνζεῦξαι σπεύδων κέλεαι σπεύδοντα καὶ αὐτόν,

ὧδε μάτην σῆς αὐτὸς ἐϋτυχίης πολεμίζων;

δέξεαι ὡς ναύτης φρεσὶ μόρσιμον αὐτίκα φόρτον,

καὶ τὸ νομιζόμενόν σοι ἐπέσσεται, ἄχθεϊ βρῖθον

ὡς παγετός, ζωῆς δ' ὅσον οὐχ ὑπὸ βένθεα δῦνον.

ὦ βροτοὶ εὐτυχέες, τῶν ἐν φρεσὶ δαιμονίη φλὸξ

οὐδὲ καταψυχθεῖσά περ ἔφθιται, ἀλλὰ πέφυκεν

ἐς βραχὺ παρμείνασα μακρὸν πόθον ἐγκαταθεῖναι.

ἢ θεὸν εὐλογίῃσιν ἐποίχομαι, εὖτε βίοιο

τοῦ πρὶν ἔχω μνήμην· οὐ μὴν τόσον εἴνεκα κείνων

ὧν τις ἔμελλε μάλιστ', οὐ τέρψιος αὐτονόμοιο,

οὐδὲ νόου παίδων εὐηθέος οἷς φιλοέργοις

εἴτ' ἀργοῖς κέαρ ἐλπὶς ὑπόπτερος ἄρτι πατάσσει·

Nor for these I raise

The song of thanks and praise;

But for those obstinate questionings

Of sense and outward things,

Fallings from us, vanishings;

Blank misgivings of a creature

Moving about in worlds not realised,

High instincts before which our mortal Nature

Did tremble like a guilty thing surprised:

But for those first affections,

Those shadowy recollections,

Which, be they what they may,

Are yet the fountain light of all our day,

Are yet a master light of all our seeing;

Uphold us, cherish, and have power to make

Our noisy years seem moments in the being

Of the eternal Silence: truths that wake,

To perish never:

Which neither listlessness, nor mad endeavour,

οὐ διὰ κεῖν' ἀνέβη παιὰν ἐμὸς ἀλλ' ἐπὶ τούτοις,
οὕνεκ', ὅσ' αἰσθήσει τις φράζεται, οὐκ ἀποκάμνει
ταῦτ' ἐς ἔλεγχον ἄγων, κεἰ κάρτα πεφυκότ' ἀπορρεῖν
πρὶν καταληφθῆναι φροῦδ' οἴχεται· οὕνεκά θ' αὑτῷ
πᾶς τις ἄπιστος ἀλᾶται ἀμήχανος, ἀμφιπολεύων
ληπτὰ μὲν οὐ περίληπτα δ', ἀνήρ τ' ἐπὶ θεῖα προβαίνων
δαιμόνιόν τι πέπονθε, παθὼν δ' ἄρα δείματι φρίσσει
ὥσθ' ὅτε τις φωρᾶται ἀτασθαλίης ἐπιχειρῶν·
ταῦτ' ἄγαμαι καὶ τοῦτό γ', ὁθούνεκα γιγνομένοισιν
εὐθὺς ἔρως τις ἀμαύρ' ὑπομιμνήσκων ἐνυπάρχει,
ὧν ἀσαφὴς τίς ἄρ' ἐστί, φάους δ' οὖν ὅσσον ὁρῶμεν
ἄρχων τ' ὀρνυμένου καὶ ὀρωρότος ἡγεμονεύων·
ὅς θ' ἡμᾶς ἀνέχει τε τροφῆς τ' ἀγανῇσιν ἀτάλλει
καὶ δύναται τόσον ὥστε βροτῶν αἰῶνα φανῆναι
ἀθανάτων βιότοιο μέρος τι βράχιστον ἐόντα,
εὐφήμου κελαδεινόν, ἐφήμερον ἀλλήκτοιο·
τοῖος ἔρως ἰδέας ἀψευδέας αἰὲν ἐόντων
ἐν φρεσὶν οὐκέτ' ἔπειτ' ἀφανιζομένας ἀναφαίνει
καὶ τόνδ' οὐκ ἀμέλει', οὐκ οἰστροδόνητος ἐφορμή,

Nor Man nor Boy,
Nor all that is at enmity with joy,
Can utterly abolish or destroy!
        Hence in a season of calm weather
        Though inland far we be,
Our Souls have sight of that immortal sea
    Which brought us hither,
        Can in a moment travel thither,
And see the Children sport upon the shore,
And hear the mighty waters rolling evermore.

                          x.

Then sing, ye Birds, sing, sing a joyous song!
        And let the young Lambs bound
        As to the tabor's sound!
We in thought will join your throng,
        Ye that pipe and ye that play,
        Ye that through your hearts to-day
        Feel the gladness of the May!

οὐκ ἀνδρῶν φύσις, οὐ παίδων, οὐκ εἴ τι κατέστη

δύσφρον ἐϋφροσύνῃσι, πανώλεθρον ἐξαλαπάξει.

τοὔνεκ᾽ ἄρ᾽ ἀκραιφνὴς νεφελῶν ὅτε πέπταται αἴθρη

καίπερ ἄνω μάλα βάντες ὅμως φρεσὶν εἰσορόωμεν

ἄφθιτον ὃν πλώσαντες ἐκέλσαμεν ἐνθάδε πόντον,

ῥίμφα τ᾽ ἐκεῖσε ποτώμεθ᾽ ἐπ᾽ ἠϊόνεσσί τε παῖδας

δερκόμεθ᾽ οἳ ποιέουσιν ἀθύρματα νηπιέῃσιν,

οἶδμά τ᾽ ἄφραστον, ἄπαυστον ἐπησθόμεθ᾽ ὠκεανοῖο.

ἀλλ᾽ ἄγετ᾽ οὖν εὔθυμον ἀείδετ᾽ ἀείδετ᾽ ἀοιδὴν

ὄρνιθες, ποσί τ᾽ ἄρνες ὁμοῦ νέαι οἷον ὑπ᾽ αὐλῶν

σκαίρετ᾽· ἐν ὑμετέρῳ δὲ χορῷ κεἰ μὴ ποσὶν ἡμεῖς

ἀλλὰ νόῳ γ᾽ οὖν κοινὰ χορεύσομεν οἵ τ᾽ αὐλεῖτε

οἷς τε μέλει παίζειν οἵ τ᾽ ἐν φρεσὶ σήμερον ἴστε

μειλίχιον θέρεος στέργηθρον ἐνισταμένοιο.

What though the radiance which was once so bright
Be now for ever taken from my sight,
　　Though nothing can bring back the hour
Of splendour in the grass, of glory in the flower;
　　　　We will grieve not, rather find
　　　　Strength in what remains behind;
　　　　In the primal sympathy
　　　　Which having been must ever be;
　　　　In the soothing thoughts that spring
　　　　Out of human suffering;
　　　　In the faith that looks through death,
In years that bring the philosophic mind.

XI.

And O, ye Fountains, Meadows, Hills, and Groves,
Forebode not any severing of our loves!
Yet in my heart of hearts I feel your might;
I only have relinquished one delight

εἶτα τί δεῖ γοάαν κεἰ μηκέτ᾽ ἐπόψομαι αἴγλην

τὴν τότε μαρμαρόεσσαν, ἔπεισί τε μήποτ᾽ ὀπίσσω

κεῖνος ἐμοὶ χρόνος αὖθις ὅτ᾽ ἀγρονόμῳ θεόσεπτος

ἐν ποίῃ τις ἔλαμπεν ἔλαμπε δ᾽ ἐπ᾽ ἄνθεσιν αὐγή;

οὐ ποθέειν χρὴ φροῦδ᾽ ἀλλ᾽ ἐρρῶσθαι φρονέοντας

ὅσσα μένει· τοίη θνητοῖσι πρὸς ἄμβροτα μίμνει

πρώταρχος φιλότης ἥ τ᾽ ὡς γέγον᾽ αἰὲν ἂν εἴη·

μίμνουσιν δὲ βροτοῖς ἐκ πημονέων παλίνορτοι

φροντίδες ἡδύπνοοι, πίστις μένει ἥ τε δέδορκε

καὶ τὸ πέρην θανάτοιο, μένουσι παρηγορέοντες

σωφρονέειν ἀδόλοισι παρηγορίῃς ἐνιαυτοί.

μή νύ τοι, ὦ κρῆναι καὶ πίσε᾽ ὄρη τε νάπαι τε

ἔλπετ᾽ ἔθ᾽ ὡς φιλέοντες ἀφησόμεθ᾽ ἀντιφιλεύντων·

νῦν γὰρ ἔθ᾽ ὑμετέροις χαίρω μάλα κήροθι θέλκτροις·

εἰ δὲ μιῆς παρέηκά τι τέρψιος, ἀλλ᾽ ἐπαοιδῆς

To live beneath your more habitual sway.

I love the Brooks which down their channels fret,

Even more than when I tripped lightly as they;

The innocent brightness of a new-born Day

      Is lovely yet;

The Clouds that gather round the setting sun

Do take a sober colouring from an eye

That hath kept watch o'er man's mortality;

Another race hath been, and other palms are won.

Thanks to the human heart by which we live,

Thanks to its tenderness, its joys, and fears,

To me the meanest flower that blows can give

Thoughts that do often lie too deep for tears.

                 WORDSWORTH.

ζῶ συνεχῶς. ἔτι μᾶλλον ὑπήκοος ὑμετερῆσι.

τὼς γὰρ ἐμοὶ φίλα ῥεῖθρα τὰ παφλάζει κατ᾽ ἐναύλους

ὥσπερ ὅτ᾽ ἴσ᾽ αὐτοῖς ἐλαφρῷ ποδὶ καὐτὸς ἐπήδων·

ἱμερόεσσα δ᾽ ἔτ᾽ ἔστ᾽ ἄκακος νέον ὀρνυμένοιο

ἤματος ἀγλαΐη· νεφέλαι δὲ ταὶ ἠελίοιο

ἀμφὶ δύσεις συνάγονται ἔμοιγε πρέπουσ᾽ ὁρόωντι

σεμνότεραί τινες ἤδη, ὃς οὐ κέκμηκα θεωρῶν

ἄθλους θνητογενῶν· ἅμα γὰρ δρόμον ἀνδράσιν ἔγνων

ἄλλον ἔχοντα τέλος στεφάνων τε λελογχότας ἄλλους.

ἦ κραδίῃ χάριν οἶδα τροφῷ θνητοῖσι βίοιο,

μειλιχίῃ κραδίῃ, φιλογηθέϊ, δειματοέσσῃ

ὡς ἐμὲ δὴ θάμ᾽ ἐπῆρεν ὃ φαυλότατον βρύει ἀνθῶν

κρέσσονα καὶ δακρύων μελεδήματα βυσσοδομεύειν.

Epitaph on a Jacobite.

To my true king I offered free from stain
Courage and faith; vain faith, and courage vain.
For him, I threw lands, honours, wealth, away,
And one dear hope, that was more prized than they.
For him I languished in a foreign clime,
Grey-haired with sorrow in my manhood's prime;
Heard on Lavernia Scargill's whispering trees,
And pined by Arno for my lovelier Tees;

ΕΠΙΤΥΜΒΙΟΝ.

πίστιν ἐγὼ Βασιλεῖ μετὰ καρτερίας ἀκέραιον,
  ᾧ θέμις ἦν, ἐτέλουν, δῶρ' ἀνόνητα τελῶν·
τοῦδ' ὕπερ ὅσσα τ' ἐμοὶ πατέρες λάχον ἧκα κατ' οὖρον,
  ἐλπίδα θ' ἣ κείνων ἦν μία πρεσβύτερον·
τοῦδ' ἕνεκ' ἐν ξείνῃ κατέδων κέαρ ἄλγεα πάσχον,
  ἡλικίας ἐν ἀκμῇ κρᾶτα φορῶν πολιόν·
πάτρια δένδρα νάπαις μοι ἐν ἀλλοδαπαῖς ψιθύριζε,
  πὰρ δὲ καλοῖς ποταμοῖς καλλιτέρους ἐπόθουν·

Beheld each night my home in fevered sleep,

Each morning started from the dream to weep ;

Till God, who saw me tried too sorely, gave

The resting place I asked, an early grave.

Oh thou, whom chance leads to this nameless stone,

From that proud country which was once mine own,

By those white cliffs I never more must see,

By that dear language which I spake like thee,

Forget all feuds, and shed one English tear

O'er English dust.   A broken heart lies here.

MACAULAY.

νυκτὸς ἀεὶ νοσεροῖς ἐν ὀνείρασι πατρίδ᾽ ἑώρων,
    ἐκ δὲ θορὼν ὕπνου κλαῖον ἑῷος ἀεί·
ἔστε Θεός μ᾽ ὑπὲρ αἶσαν ἄχει βεβολημένον εἰδὼς
    παῦσε, πάροιθ᾽ ὥρας δοὺς χατέοντι θανεῖν.
ὦ ξέν᾽, ὅτῳ συνέβη τόδε σῆμ᾽ ἐπ᾽ ἀνώνυμον ἐλθεῖν
    πατρίδος ἐκ σεμνῆς ἣ τρέφε κἀμὲ πάλαι,
πρός σε πάτρας λευκᾶν ἃς οὐκέτ᾽ ἐπόψομαι ἀκτᾶν,
    γλώσσης θ᾽ ἣν ἴσα σοὶ καὐτὸς ἔχαιρον ἱείς,
τλῆθι παρεὶς στάσεων ἐσάπαξ φθόνον Ἄγγλος ἐπ᾽ Ἄγγλῳ
    δάκρυ βαλεῖν· κεῖμαι δυσφροσύνῃ φθίμενος.

[In the following series, each successive rendering of Mr W. G. Clark's quatrain was a translation from its immediate predecessor, which alone was seen by the translator. The names of Sir Richard Jebb's collaborators are as follows:

"W. G. C.": William George Clark, Fellow of Trinity College, Cambridge, and from 1857 to 1869 Public Orator in the University: co-editor with Mr W. Aldis Wright of the *Cambridge Shakespeare.*

"W. S.": William Selwyn, Lady Margaret Professor of Divinity from 1855 to 1875.

"E. D.": Emmanuel Deutsch, of the British Museum, an eminent Hebraist, and author of an article on the Talmud which appeared in the *Quarterly Review* of October 1867.

"F. L.": Frederick Locker[-Lampson], the poet.

"J. M.": J. Milsand, of Dijon, to whom Robert Browning dedicated *Sordello.*]

An Experiment in 'Polyglot Russian Scandal.'

The *Field* had announced that the beautiful Miss X., while fishing in Scotland, had landed a salmon weighing 13 lbs.

No artificial flies my fancy took,
Nature's own magic lured me to your hook:
Play me no more—no thought to 'scape have I—
But land me, land me, at your feet to die.

W. G. C.

Delia, cur mutos pisces et flumina semper,
   digna frui praeda nobiliore, colis?
ipse loquens, vocique paratus reddere vocem,
   oro te, precibus me cape capta meis:
nil opus est lino fallacem ducere muscam,
   vox tua perpetuo me trahit imperio.
desine; lusisti nimium; servatus ab undis
   collocer ante tuos emoriarque pedes.

W. S.

πρὸς τί, Χλόη, ποταμούς τε καὶ ἰχθύας αἰὲν ἀναύδους,
 ἐξὸν ἄγραις χαίρειν κρείσσοσιν, ἀμφιπολεῖς;
αὐτός, ἔχων φωνεῖν τ᾽ ἀγορευούσῃ τ᾽ ἀγορεύειν,
 ἀντιβολῶ σ᾽, αἵρει ταῖσδέ μ᾽ ἁλοῦσα λιταῖς.
μηδ᾽ ἔτι μηρίνθῳ μυίας δελέασμα παρέλκειν·
 σὸν γὰρ ἀεί μ᾽ ἕλκει φθέγμα βίᾳ προσάγον.
παῦε· λίαν γὰρ ἔπαισας· ἐγὼ δ᾽ ὑδάτων ἀποσωθεὶς
 σοῖσι προσαρθείην κἀποθάνοιμι ποσίν.

R. C. J.

Wie doch, o Chloe, um Flüsse und Fische, ewiglich
 schweigsam
  —Harret doch edler Wild Dein!—wandelst Du stetig
  einher?
Ich nun, mit Stimme begabt, Dir Redenden Rede zu stehen
 Flehe Dich, greife mich auf, von meinen Flehen erweicht.
Nimmer von Dir bedarf es der fliegenbeköderten Angel,
 Zieht ja Dein Ton fürwahr Dir mich mit Allgewalt nach.
O lass ab! Allzulang tändelst Du. Fänd ich nur, fluthbefreit,
 endlich
  Von Deinen Händen erfasst, zu Deinen Füssen den Tod.

E. D.

Pourquoi, ta ligne en main et le front en sueur,
  Fatiguer ton beau corps à courir sur la rive ?
Qu'as-tu besoin de mouche, et d'hameçon trompeur ?
                              Enfant naïve,
Une plus noble proie est là qui s'offre à toi,
  Dis un mot, et pour voir dans un œil un sourire,
J'accours du fond des eaux.   Que tardes-tu ?   Prends-moi !
  Et, pressé dans tes mains, à tes pieds que j'expire.

                                   J. M.

Why rod in hand and glowing, why ?
  My simple little dear,
What need have you with hook and fly
  To come a-fishing here ?
Smile but one smile, I'll gladly do
  Much more than you desire ;
I'll swim to you—and quickly, too—
  And at your feet expire.

                                   F. L.

SOPRA IL MONUMENTO DI DANTE

CHE SI PREPARAVA IN FIRENZE.

Perchè le nostre genti

Pace sotto le bianche ali raccolga,

Non fien da' lacci sciolte

Dell' antico sopor l' itale menti

S' ai patrii esempi della prisca etade

Questa terra fatal non si rivolga.

ΤΟΙΣ ΠΑΡΑΣΚΕΥΑΖΟΜΕΝΟΙΣ

ΤΟ ΕΝ ΦΛΩΡΕΝΤΙΑΙ ΤΟΥ ΔΑΝΤΕ ΜΝΗΜΕΙΟΝ.

γᾶν μὲν Εἰρήνα πτερύγεσσιν ὑπαὶ λευκαῖς ἔχει   στρ. α΄
τάνδ᾽· ἀλλὰ πῶς ῥήξαισα πανώλεος ὕπνου
δεσμὰ πατρὶς τᾶς χρονίας ἀϝάτας εὔξαιτό κεν ἐξαναδῦμεν,
τῶν πάλαι εὐδοκίμων εἰ μὴ πάλιν
μναμοσύναν πατέρων
ἀνεγείροι, μορσίμῳ
συμφορᾷ κεκραμένα;

J. T.   16

O Italia, a cor ti stia

Far ai passati onor ; chè d' altrettali

Oggi vedove son le tue contrade,

Nè v' è chi d' onorar ti si convegna.

Volgiti indietro, e guarda, o patria mia,

Quella schiera infinita d' immortali,

E piangi e di te stessa ti disdegna ;

Chè senza sdegno omai la doglia è stolta :

Volgiti e ti vergogna e ti riscuoti,

E ti punga una volta

Pensier degli avi nostri e de' nepoti.

 D' aria e d' ingegno e di parlar diverso

Per lo toscano suol cercando gìa

L' ospite desioso

Dove giaccia colui per lo cui verso

Il meonio cantor non è più solo.

τὶν μεριμνᾶν, Ἰταλία, κορυφὰν τάνδ' ἐννέπω, ἀντ. α΄
τιμὰς νέμειν τοῖς οἰχομένοισι δικαίας·
οὐ γὰρ ἄνδρας τοῖσι πρὶν ἀντιπάλους ταῖς σαῖς ἔθ' ὁρᾷς ἐν
        ἀρούραις,
οὐδ' ἱκανόν τινα σὰν αὔξειν φάτιν.
ἀλλ' ἐπὶ τοὺς φθιμένους
ἀπὸ τῶν νῦν ἔμπαλιν
τρέψον, ὦ πάτρα, νόον·

κείνων δ' ἀπέραντον ἰδοῖσ' ἵλαν, ὅσοις ἐπ. α΄
κῦδος ἀγήραον ἀνθεῖ, δάκρυσι δευομένα
γνῶθι τάλαιν' ἵν' ἀτιμίας μόλες·
νῦν γὰρ ἀνωφελὲς ἄλγος,
ᾧ τινι μὴ κέαρ αἰσχύνας ἅμα κέντρον ἐπείγῃ.
κεῖσε βλέποισα καταισχύνου τε καὶ ὄρσο, διδαχθεῖσ' εἰσάπαξ
ἁλίκ' ἔργ' ἀραμένων προγόνων
οἵαν ἐπαίδευσας σποράν.

πατρίδων μὲν παντοδαπᾶν ἄπο δεῦρ' ὁρμώμενοι στρ. β΄
ξεῖνοι, τρόπον τ' αὐδάν τ' ἀνόμοιοι, ἀοιδοῦ
σᾶμα δίζηνται, πόθι νιν κατέχει Τυρσανίδος εὐκλεὲς αἶας,
οὗ σοφίας χάριν αἰδοιεστάτας
οὐκέτι Χῖος ἀνὴρ
ἐπέων ἐν τέκτοσιν
χωρὶς ἧσται γειτόνων.

Ed, oh vergogna! udia

Che non che il cener freddo e l' ossa nude

Giaccian esuli ancora

Dopo il funereo dì sott' altro suolo,

Ma non sorgea dentro a tue mura un sasso,

Firenze, a quello per la cui virtude

Tutto il mondo t' onora.

Oh voi pietosi, onde sì tristo e basso

Obbrobrio laverà nostro paese!

Bell' opra hai tolta e di che amor ti rende,

Schiera prode e cortese,

Qualunque petto amor d' Italia accende.

    Amor d' Italia, o cari,

Amor di questa misera vi sproni,

Vêr cui pietade è morta

In ogni petto omai, perciò che amari

Giorni dopo il seren dato n' ha il cielo.

Spirti v' aggiunga e vostra opra coroni

Misericordia, o figli,

τοὶ δὲ πεύθονται λόγον ὦ πόποι αἴσχιστον κλύειν,   ἀντ. β′
ὡς ἐν ξένᾳ ψυχρὰ κόνις ὀστέα τ᾽ ἀνδρὸς
γυμνὰ κείνου κᾶτι μένει, φυγάδος πάτρας ἀπάνευθε ταφέντος,
οὐδέ τί Ϝοι κτίσας, ὦ Φλωρεντία,
μνᾶμα, δι᾽ οὗ μεγάλαν
ἀρετὰν αὐτὰ πρέπεις
πᾶσιν ἔνδοξος βροτοῖς.

ὦ κτησάμενοι πραπίδων ἐξαίρετον   ἐπ. β′
εὐσεβίαν, χάριν ὧν κηλῖδος ἔτι στυγερᾶς
νίψεται ἅδε μελαμπαγὲς μύσος
χθὼν ὁσίοισι καθαρμοῖς,
ἔργματος ἴστε καλοῦ θέντες βάθρον, αἰδόφρον ἴλα,
φροντίδος οἷον ἀπ᾽ εὐψύχου παρὰ πᾶσιν ἐπαίνου τεύξεται,
οἷς γ᾽ ἐνὶ στήθεσιν Ἰταλίας
μὴ πᾶς κατέσβαχ᾽ ἵμερος.

ὔμμε δ᾽, ὦ γενναιότατοι, τόδ᾽ ἐπ᾽ ἔργμ᾽ ὡρμαμένους   στρ. γ′
στέργηθρα γᾶς παμπειθέα τᾶσδ᾽ ἐποτρύνοι
τᾶς ἄγαν δυσδαίμονος, ἇς σέβας ἤδη πᾶσι φρενῶν ἀπόλωλεν,
ἀνίκα τᾶς προτέρας ἐξ εὐδίας
κλαρονόμους ἀχέων
πόρε δαίμων ἀμέρας·
ματρὸς ὧν υἱοὶ χάριν

E duolo e sdegno di cotanto affanno

Onde bagna costei le guance e il velo.

Ma voi di quale ornar parola o canto

Si debbe, a cui non pur cure o consigli,

Ma dell' ingegno e della man daranno

I sensi e le virtudi eterno vanto

Oprate e mostre nella dolce impresa?

Quali a voi note invio, sì che nel core,

Sì che nell' alma accesa

Nova favilla indurre abbian valore?

  Voi spirerà l' altissimo subbietto,

Ed acri punte premeravvi al seno.

Chi dirà l' onda e il turbo

Del furor vostro e dell' immenso affetto?

Chi pingerà l' attonito sembiante?

Chi degli occhi il baleno?

Qual può voce mortal celeste cosa

Agguagliar figurando?

τᾶσδε κοινὰν πάντες ὁμόφρονος ἐν βουλᾶς ἀκμᾷ   ἀντ. γ´
τολμᾶτε τοῦδ᾽ ἔργου κορυφαῖς ἐπιβᾶμεν,
πατρίδος δ᾽, οἵᾳ συνέκυρσε, νεμεσσάθητ᾽ ἐσιδόντες ἀνίαν,
ἇς καὶ ἕκατι παρειάς τ᾽ ἔμπεδον
ἁ κακοποτμοτάτα
δακρύων ἁβρὰς ἄχνᾳ
καὶ καλύπτραν τέγγεται.

τίς δὴ λόγος ἢ τίς ἀοιδὰ δαιδάλου   ἐπ. γ´
τέκτονος ὕμμι πρεπόντως ἁρμόσει, ἄφθιτον οἷς
δόξαν ἄγει φιλόφρων τ᾽ εὐβουλία
καὶ σύνεσις πολύμητις
χείρ θ᾽ ἅμ᾽ ἀριστόπονος λαμπρά τε καλὸν φύσις οἷμον
ἱεμένα; τίνα πέμπων ὕμμι μεγασθενέος Φοίβου νόμον
μεῖζον ἄρω μένος ἐσσυμένοις
σπουδάν τ᾽ ἐπιφλέξω φρενῶν;

αὐτὸ μὰν ἀρκεῖ χρέος οὗ καὶ ἀγωνίζεσθ᾽ ὕπερ   στρ. δ´
ὥστ᾽ ὀξέα ψυχαῖς ὑπὸ κέντρα δονῆσαι·
τίς κεν εἴποι κῦμα μέγ᾽ ὑμετέρας χειμῶνά τ᾽ ἀθέσφατον ὁρμᾶς,
δέργμα τίς ἔνθεον ὄσσων τ᾽ ἀστραπάς;
χρῆμα γὰρ οὐράνιον
πόθεν ἂν θνατῶν φάτις
γαρύοι; θεῖος δ᾽ ἔρως

Lunge sia, lunge alma profana. Oh quante

Lacrime al nobil sasso Italia serba!

Come cadrà? come dal tempo rósa

Fia vostra gloria o quando?

Voi, di che il nostro mal si disacerba,

Sempre vivete, o care arti divine,

Conforto a nostra sventurata gente,

Fra l' itale ruine

Gl' itali pregi a celebrare intente.

  Ecco voglioso anch' io

Ad onorar nostra dolente madre

Porto quel che mi lice,

E mesco all' opra vostra il canto mio,

Sedendo u' vostro ferro i marmi avviva.

O dell' etrusco metro inclito padre,

Se di cosa terrena,

εἴ τιν᾽ οὗτος μηδὲν ἔθελξε, χοροῦ τοῦδ᾽ ἐκποδὼν   ἀντ. δ᾽
στᾶμεν προφωνῶ. φεῦ, λίθον ὅσσ᾽ ἐπὶ κεῖνον
πένθιμον μέλλει δόσιν Ἰταλία δακρύματα πατρὶς ἐνεῖκαι·
πῶς θέμις ὔμμι ποτ᾽ ἐκλείπειν κλέος;
τίς δὲ περιπλομένων
ἐτέων εὐδοξίαν
τάνδ᾽ ἀμαυρώσει χρόνος;

τεχνᾶν βασίλειαι ἀγακλειτᾶν, ὑφ᾽ ἇν,   ἐπ. δ᾽
θεσπέσιαι Χάριτες, λωφᾷ πικρὸν ἄμμιν ἄχος,
ὔμμι μὲν ἀθάνατος ζωὰ μένει,
τλάμοσι φάρμακον ἀστοῖς
δυστυχίας ἀλεγεινᾶς, αἳ κάκ᾽ ἐς αἰνὰ πεσοίσας
Ἰταλίας ἀρετᾶν μνάμαν ἐπεγείρετε τᾶν ἐγχωριᾶν·
ματρὶ δ᾽ ἁμᾷ γέρας ἀχνυμένᾳ
κἀγὼ προσάψαι μώμενος

οἷά γ᾽ ἴσχω δῶρα πάρειμι φέρων, ὑμαῖς ἐμὰν   στρ. ε᾽
μίξαις ἀοιδὰν ἐργασίαισι ποθειναῖς,
ἀγχίτερμον ναιετάων ἕδος, οὗ καὶ καλλίτεχνοι τελέοισιν
χεῖρες ἀλίγκιον ἐμψύχῳ λίθον.
ὦ σοφίας ὕπατον
στέφανον δρέψαις πάτερ
μουσικᾶς Τυρσανίδος,

Se di costei che tanto alto locasti

Qualche novella ai vostri lidi arriva,

Io so ben che per te gioia non senti,

Chè saldi men che cera e men ch' arena,

Verso la fama che di te lasciasti,

Son bronzi e marmi; e dalle nostre menti

Se mai cadesti ancor, s' unqua cadrai,

Cresca, se crescer può, nostra sciaura,

E in sempiterni guai

Pianga tua stirpe a tutto il mondo oscura.

   Ma non per te; per questa ti rallegri

Povera patria tua, s' unqua l' esempio

Degli avi e de' parenti

Ponga ne' figli sonnacchiosi ed egri

Tanto valor che un tratto alzino il viso.

Ahi, da che lungo scempio

Vedi afflitta costei, che sì meschina

Te salutava allora

Che di novo salisti al paradiso!

πύστις εἰ κἀκεῖ τις ἐπιχθονίων, εἰ πατρίδος   ἀντ. ε´
κείνας ἱκάνει σ᾽ ἂν πολύφαμον ἔθηκας,
οὐχ ὑπὲρ σαυτοῦ, τόδ᾽ ἴσαμι καλῶς, τιμαῖς ἐπὶ ταῖσδε γέγαθας,
εἴ γ᾽ ὃ λέλοιπας ἐν ἀνθρώποις κλέος
μνᾶμα βεβαιότερον
λιθίνου θ᾽ ἱδρύματος
καὶ τύπων χαλκαλάτων

τόσσῳ τετέλεσται, ὅσῳ περ καὶ λίθου   ἐπ. ε´
ψάμμος ἀφαυρότερον χαλκοῖό τε κηρὸς ἔφυ·
εἰ δ᾽ ἔπεσες σύ ποτ᾽ ἐξ ἀμᾶν φρενῶν
ἠὲ πέσοις ἔτ᾽ ἄτιμος,
μείζονα δὴ πόροι ἀμὶν, εἴ τιν᾽ ἔχοι, κακὰ δαίμων,
σὺν δ᾽ ὀδύναις γένος ἀλλήκτοις τεὸν ἀκλεὲς ἐν θνατοῖς στένοι.
σαῖς μὲν οὐ τέρπεαι ἀγλαΐαις,
οἰκτρᾶς δ᾽ ὑπὲρ σᾶς πατρίδος,

εἰ ποτ᾽ ἀστοὶ κυδαλίμων προγόνων μεμναμένοι   στρ. ϛ´
ῥαθυμίας ἀλλαξάμενοι σθένος ἀργᾶς
κρᾶτ᾽ ἀνορθώσοντι χρόνον γ᾽ ἐπὶ παῦρον.   φεῦ· χαλεπαῖς ὅσα
   λώβαις
δαρὸν ἐλαυνομέναν λεύσσεις πάτραν,
ἅ σ᾽, ὅτ᾽ ἐς Ἠλυσίας
μακάρων ἕδρας στόλον
ἐστάλης τὸν δεύτερον,

Oggi ridotta sì che, a quel che vedi,

Fu fortunata allor donna e reina.

Tal miseria l' accora

Qual tu forse mirando a te non credi.

Taccio gli altri nemici e l' altre doglie,

Ma non la più recente e la più fera,

Per cui presso alle soglie

Vide la patria tua l' ultima sera.

    Beato te che il fato

A viver non dannò fra tanto orrore ;

Che non vedesti in braccio

L' itala moglie a barbaro soldato ;

Non predar, non guastar cittadi e cólti

L' asta inimica e il peregrin furore ;

Non degl' itali ingegni

Tratte l' opre divine a miseranda

Schiavitude oltre l' alpe, e non de' folti

οὐκ ἐν ὥρᾳ θήκατ᾽ ἀποιχόμενον· νῦν δ᾽ αὖ κακοῖς   ἀντ. ς΄
ἀλγεῖ τοιούτοις, ὥστε παρ᾽ ἂν σὺ δέδορκας
ὀλβία δόξαι τᾶς τόθ᾽ ἕκατι τύχας χώρᾳ πάρος ἐμβασιλεῦσαι·
θαῦμά κ᾽ ἄπιστον ἴσως κεῖθεν δρακεὶς
πῆμα τοσόνδε λέγοις.
τὰ μὲν ἄλλ᾽ ἐχθρούς τ᾽ ἀφεὶς
καὶ πόνους σιγάσομαι·

δεινῶν δ᾽ ὃ νεώτατον ἔχθιστόν θ᾽ ὁμῶς,   ἐπ. ς΄
τοῦτο φράσαιμ᾽ ἄν, ὑφ᾽ οὗ μοίρας ἐπιόντα τεὰ
πατρὶς ὄπωπε τελευταίας ζόφον.
ἄξιος εἶ μακαρίζειν,
ὃν πότμος οὐ κάθελεν λεύσσονθ᾽ Ὑπερίονος αὐγὰς
ταῖσδε σύνοικον ἐν ἄταις ἔμμεναι, οὐδ᾽ ἀκολάστους προσβλέπειν
ἀγκάλας ἀμφιτιθέντα βίᾳ
νύμφαισιν αἰχματὰν ξένον

Ἰταλαῖς· οὐδ᾽ εἴσιδες ἄστεα καὶ λευρούς γύας   στρ. ζ΄
ὠμᾶς βιατᾶν ἀλλοδαπῶν ὑπὸ λύσσας
δαΐοις ἐν δούρασι περθομένους, ἔργων θ᾽ ὅσ᾽ ὑπέρτατα τέχναις
Ἰταλικαὶ Χάριτες θείαις κάμον
ἑλκόμεν᾽ εἰς ὕποχον
Βορέᾳ γᾶν, βαρβάρων
δεσποτᾶν κόσμον δόμοις·

Carri impedita la dolente via;

Non gli aspri cenni ed i superbi regni;

Non udisti gli oltraggi e la nefanda

Voce di libertà che ne schernia

Tra il suon delle catene e de' flagelli.

Chi non si duol? che non soffrimmo? intatto

Che lasciaron quei felli?

Qual tempio, quale altare o qual misfatto?

   Perchè venimmo a sì perversi tempi?

Perchè il nascer ne desti o perchè prima

Non ne desti il morire,

Acerbo fato? onde a stranieri ed empi

Nostra patria vedendo ancella e schiava

E da mordace lima

Roder la sua virtù, di null' aita

E di nullo conforto

Lo spietato dolor che la stracciava

Ammollir ne fu dato in parte alcuna.

οὐδ' ἀμαξᾶν πλήρε' ἴδες πυκινᾶν λυγρὰν ὁδόν,   ἀντ. ζ′
ξείνων ὄπ' οὐκ ἄκουσας ἀμείλιχον ἀστοῖς
ἐντολὰς κραίνοισαν ὑπερφιάλους, δούλοις τ' ὄνυμ', ὥσπερ ἐφ'
    ὕβρει,
σεμνὸν Ἐλευθερίας, χειρωμάτων
δυσσεβέων πρόφασιν,
ἀνακαρυχθέν, πεδᾶν
ἔν τε μαστίγων ψόφῳ.

τίς πένθεος οὐ μετέχει; ποῖον δ' ἄχος   ἐπ. ζ′
οὐ φέρομεν; τί δ' ἀπόρθητον νοέοισιν ἐᾶν
οἶδ' ἄνομοι, τί θεῶν ἀνάκτορον
ἢ τίνα βωμὸν ὑβρισταί;
ποῖα κάκ' οὐ τελέοισ'; εἴθ' ὤφελε μή ποθ' ἱκέσθαι
σκαιοσύναν ἐπὶ τοιαύταν γένος ἀμόν· ἰώ, ζωὰν τί δή,
πικρὲ δαῖμον, πόρες ἄμμιν ἔχειν,
ἀλλ' οὐ φθάσαις Ἀΐδου τέλος;

ἀλλοφύλοις ὧν ἀθέοις ὑπακούοισαν πάτραν,   στρ. η′
δούλαν τιν' ὥς, ἀστῶν τ' ἀρετὰν ὑπ' ἀνάγκας
εἰσορῶντες τειρομέναν δακεθύμοι', οὔτε τιν' ἄμμες ἀρωγὰν
οὔτε παραγορίαν ἔμπας φέρειν
ἄθλιοι ἀρκέσαμεν,
ὀδύνας θελκτήριον
τᾶς διανταίας ἄκος.

Ahi non il sangue nostro e non la vita

Avesti, o cara; e morto

Io non son per la tua cruda fortuna.

Qui l' ira al cor, qui la pietade abbonda:

Pugnò, cadde gran parte anche di noi:

Ma per la moribonda

Italia no; per li tiranni suoi.

   Padre, se non ti sdegni,

Mutato sei da quel che fosti in terra.

Morian per le rutene

Squallide piagge, ahi d' altra morte degni,

Gl' itali prodi; e lor fea l' aere e il cielo

E gli uomini e le belve immensa guerra.

Cadeano a squadre a squadre

Semivestiti, maceri e cruenti,

Ed era letto agli egri corpi il gelo.

Allor, quando traean l' ultime pene,

Membrando questa desiata madre,

ὦ φίλα θρέπτειρα, σέθεν δ' ὕπερ οὐκ ἔτλα θανεῖν   ἀντ. η′
ψυχάν τις αἰχμαῖς ἀνδροφόνοισι προτείνων·
σαῖσι δ' ἐν λώβαις σόος εἴμ'. ἑλέτω θυμὸν χόλος ἠδὲ καὶ οἶκτος,
οὕνεκα μαρνάμενοι πλεῖστοι πέσον
οὐχ ὑπὲρ Ἰταλικᾶς
φθινάδος γᾶς Ἰταλοί,
ἀλλὰ τῶν κείνᾳ ζυγὸν

ἔχθιστον ἐπ' αὐχένι θέντων. ὦ πάτερ   ἐπ. η′
ἁμετέρων μέγ' ἀοιδῶν ἔξοχε, ταῦτ' ἐπιδὼν
εἰ σὺ χόλῳ φρένα μὴ δάκνει, φύσιν
ἦ ῥα νέαν μεταμεῖψαι
φαμί σε τᾶς προτέρας ἂν ζωὸς ἐών ποτ' ἔφαινες·
τηλεπόρου γὰρ ἀπώλοντο Σκυθίας καθ' ὁδοὺς δυστερπέας
Ἰταλῶν φέρτατοι, οὔ τι τύχας,
αἰαῖ, τοιαύτας ἄξιοι·

τοῖς ἁμᾷ δυσχείμερος ἄλγεα πόρσυν' οὐρανός,   στρ. θ′
ἀνδρῶν δ' ἁμᾷ θηρῶν τ' ἀπερείσιος ὕβρις·
ἡμίγυμνοι δ' ὡς χαμαὶ ἰσχνὰ μέλη, χρανθέντα φοναῖσι, κατ' ἴλας
θέσσαν, ὑπῆν νοσεροῖς πάχνα λέχος.
ἀλλ' ὅτε δή σφιν ἄγεν
Ἀΐδας τέρμ' ἔσχατον,
φιλτάτας μεμναμένοι

Diceano: oh non le nubi e non i venti,

Ma ne spegnesse il ferro, e per tuo bene,

O patria nostra. Ecco da te rimoti,

Quando più bella a noi l' età sorride,

A tutto il mondo ignoti,

Moriam per quella gente che t' uccide.

Di lor querela il boreal deserto

E conscie fur le sibilanti selve.

Così vennero al passo,

E i negletti cadaveri all' aperto

Su per quello di neve orrido mare

Dilacerâr le belve;

E sarà il nome degli egregi e forti

Pari mai sempre ed uno

Con quel de' tardi e vili. Anime care,

Bench' infinita sia vostra sciagura,

Datevi pace; e questo vi conforti

Che conforto nessuno

Avrete in questa o nell' età futura.

In seno al vostro smisurato affanno

Posate, o di costei veraci figli,

ματρὸς εἶπον· φεῦ, τί κελαινεφέων πορθούμενοι   ἀντ. θ′
πλαγαῖς θυελλᾶν θνᾴσκομεν, οἷσι προσῆκεν,
ὦ πάτρα, σοῦ καδομένοισι πεσεῖν χάρμαις ἐνὶ κυδιανείραις;
νῦν δ᾽, ἐρατῶπις ὅτ᾽ αἰὼν προσγελᾷ,
φθειρόμεθ᾽ οἵδε σέθεν
δίχα, παντᾷ νώνυμοι,
σῶν ὑπὲρ λυμαντόρων.

τοιαῦτ᾽ ὀλοφυρομένων κρυσταλλοπὰξ   ἐπ. θ′
ἄϊε γαῖα λιγύφθογγοί τ᾽ ἀνέμοισι νάπαι.
τάνδε βίου μὲν ἀπαλλαγὰν λάχον·
σώματα δ᾽ οἰκτρὰ θανόντων
ἂμ πεδίων χιονοβλήτους πλάκας ὀκρυοέσσας
δάπτον ὑπαίθρια θῆρες· δόξα δ᾽ ἴσα τὸν ἔπειτ᾽ αἰεὶ χρόνον
τοῖσι λαμπροῖς ἀγαθοῖς θ᾽ ἔπεται,
δειλοί θ᾽ ὁμοίως εἴ τινες

ἦσαν αὐτῶν καὶ κακοί. ὦ μεγαλᾶν δὴ συμφορᾶν   στρ. ι′
κύρσαντες ἔμπας στέργετε· πήμασι δ᾽ εἴπερ
μήτε νῦν μήτ᾽ εἰσοπίσω ποτὲ παιὼν ὑμετέροισι πελάσσει,
τλᾶτε τόδ᾽ αὐτὸ μαθόντες καρτερεῖν.
σῖγα τρέφοντες ἄχος
ἀνέχεσθ᾽ ἐξαίσιον,
γνήσι᾽ ὦ τέκν᾽ ἀθλίας

Al cui supremo danno

Il vostro solo è tal che s' assomigli.

   Di voi già non si lagna

La patria vostra, ma di chi vi spinse

A pugnar contra lei,

Sì ch' ella sempre amaramente piagna

E il suo col vostro lacrimar confonda.

O di costei ch' ogni altra gloria vinse

Pietà nascesse in core

A tal de' suoi ch' affaticata e lenta

Di sì buia vorago e sì profonda

La ritraesse! O glorioso spirto,

Dimmi: d' Italia tua morto è l' amore?

Dì: quella fiamma che t' accese, è spenta?

Dì: nè più mai rinverdirà quel mirto

Ch' alleggiò per gran tempo il nostro male?

Nostre corone al suol fien tutte sparte?

Nè sorgerà mai tale

Che ti rassembri in qualsivoglia parte?

ματρός, ᾇ πάντων ὑπάτοισι δαμασθείσᾳ πόνοις   ἀντ. ι′
οὐκ ἔστι πλὴν ὑμῶν ὃς ὁμοῖα πέπονθεν.
οὐ γὰρ ὑμῖν μέμφεται Ἰταλία, κείνῳ δ' ὃς ἐπῶρσ' ἀέκοντας
πατρίδι δύσθεος ἀντᾶραι μάχαν·
ὧν ἕνεκ' ἀχθομένα
δρόσον αἰεὶ δακρύων
ὕμμι κοινὰν εἴβεται.

πῶς ἂν πολυπήμονος αἰδῶ πατρίδος   ἐπ. ι′
τᾶς πρὶν ὑπείροχον ἄλλων κῦδος ἀειραμένας
ἐν πραπίδεσσι λάβοι τις ἐκγόνων,
ὅς κ' ἐρύσαιτο κλύδωνος
ἐκ μέλανος βαθυδίνου τριβομέναν καμάτοισιν;
εἰπέ μοι, ὦ μακάρων τιμαῖσιν ἀοιδὲ μιγεὶς ὑψιθρόνοις,
ἆρα σᾶς οἴχεται Ἰταλίας
πρόρριζος ἐκ θνατῶν ἔρως;

ἆρ' ἀπέσβακ' ἔνθεος ἃ σὲ κατεῖχ' ὁρμὰ φρενῶν,   στρ. κ′
οὐδ' αὖθις ἁμᾶν, ὡς τὸ πάροιθ', ὀδυνάων
μαλθακὸν κούφισμα φέροισ' ἀναθαλήσει ποτ' ἐν ἀνδράσι μύρτος;
ἆρα χαμαιπετέων ἄμμι φθίνει
πᾶσα χάρις στεφάνων,
παρόμοιον δ' οὐδαμοῦ
σοί τιν' αὖ θρέψει πατρίς;

In eterno perimmo? e il nostro scorno

Non ha verun confine?

Io mente viva andrò sclamando intorno:

Volgiti agli avi tuoi, guasto legnaggio;

Mira queste ruine

E le carte e le tele e i marmi e i templi;

Pensa qual terra premi; e se destarti

Non può la luce di cotanti esempli,

Che stai? lèvati e parti.

Non si conviene a sì corrotta usanza

Questa d' animi eccelsi altrice e scola:

Se di codardi è stanza,

Meglio l' è rimaner vedova e sola.

LEOPARDI.

ἦ ῥ᾿ ἐσαεὶ κείμεθα; μέτρον ἄρ᾿ οὐκ ἔσται ψόγου;   ἀντ. κ΄
ζωᾶς ἔγωγ᾿ ἔστ᾿ ἂν μετέχω, τάδε παντᾷ
πᾶσι καρύξω· προγόνων ἀρετᾶς μνάσασθε, γένος πολὺ χεῖρον·
λείψαν᾿ ὁρᾶτε τάδ᾿ ὧν κεῖνοι κάμον,
Πιερίδων τ᾿ ἐρατᾶν
μελέτας ἱστῶν θ᾿ ὑφὰς
ἔργα τ᾿ εὐμόρφων λίθων

ναούς τε θεῶν· χθονὸς ἴσθ᾿ οἵας πέδον   ἐπ. κ΄
στείβετε· κυδαλίμων δ᾿ εἰ πᾶν φάος ἐκ πατέρων
ὕμμι μάταν κέχυται, ποῖ χρὴ μένειν;
ἔκτοποι ἔρρετε γαίας·
οὐ γὰρ ἔοικεν ἀνάνδροις θρέμμασι πατρίδ᾿ ὁμιλεῖν
ἃ μεγαλόφρονα παίδευσ᾿· εἰ δὲ γενήσεται ἀψύχων λιμήν,
κρέσσον᾿ αἶσάν κε λαχοῖσα πέλοι
χήρα τ᾿ ἐρήμα τ᾿ εἰσαεί.

ΤΩΙ ΕΝ ΒΟΝΩΝΙΑΙ ΠΑΝΕΠΙΣΤΗΜΙΩΙ

ΕΚΑΤΟΝΤΑΕΤΗΡΙΔΟΣ ΟΓΔΟΗΣ ΕΟΡΤΗΝ ΑΓΟΝΤΙ.

Μᾶτερ ἀρχαία σοφίας, ὅθεν Εὐρώπᾳ πάλαι   στρ. α΄
τᾶς ὀρθοβούλου φῶς Θέμιτος νέον ὦρτο,
ἐργμάτων ἴαμα βιαιοτάτων, στυγνᾶν ἐλατήριον ἀτᾶν,
Εὐνομίας ἀγανὸς κάρυξ βροτοῖς,
χείματος ὡς δνοφεροῦ
ὅτε φοινικάνθεμον
ἦρ πεδάμειψαν γύαι,

φαιδίμας χαῖρ' Ἰταλίας θύγατερ, τὰν ἀστέων   ἀντ. α'
πρέσβιστον ἐξ ἄλλων ἐφίλασεν Ἀθάνα,
παῖς θ' ὁ Λατοίδας, ὅ τ' ἐλευθερίᾳ χαίρων πολιάοχος Ἑρμᾶς·
νῦν σε μάλ' ἀδυπνόοις δαιδαλλέμεν
καίριον εὐλογίαις,
ὅθ' ἑορτᾶς γένεαι
παντοσέμνου χάρματος·

Ὧραι γὰρ ἐπερχόμεναι θνατοῖς Διὸς   ἐπ. α'
εἰς ἑκατοντάδας ὀκτὼ δὴ τελέας ἐτέων
δόξαν ἐϋστέφανον Βονωνίας
μαρτυρέοντι γεγάκειν·
τᾷ καὶ ἀγαλλόμεναι ξείνων πολυγαθέες ἶλαι
παντοδαπᾶν ἀπὸ πεμφθεῖσαι πολίων ποτινίσονθ' ἑστίαν
φιλτάταν Πιερίδεσσι, τεὰν
κοινᾷ κλεΐξοισαι χάριν.

φαντὶ Τυρσανοὺς μὲν ἀρηϊφίλους κτίσσαι βάθροις   στρ. β'
ἐν τοῖσδε Φελσίναν, ὅθι χεῦμα Σαβάνας
γείτονος Ῥήνῳ πεδίον βρέχει Ἀπεννινόθεν εὐρυμέτωπον,
πίονα δῶρα τρέφον Δαμάτερος
οὐδ' ἀπαδὸν Βρομίῳ·
ὅσα δ' ἔστ' Αἰνειαδᾶν
ἐν λόγοις, σιγάσομαι·

Μοῖσα, τὶν δ' ἀρχὰ γλυκερῶν ὑποκείσθω φθεγμάτων,   ἀντ. β'
τηλοῦ τις ὡς στίλβων ἀριδείκετος ἀστήρ,
οὐκ ἀμαυρωθὲν γενεαῖς ἅμα πολλαῖσιν κλέος Ἰρνερίοιο[1]·
λαμπάδα κεῖνος ἀνέσχ' ὀρθὰν Δίκας,
σπέρματα βαιὰ πυρὸς
ἀνεγείραις κείμενα
δαρὸν ἐν ψυχρᾷ σποδῷ·

τεθμῶν ὃς ἄνοιξε θεοδμάτων ὁδοὺς   ἐπ. β'
τοὺς ὁ μεγιστόπολις Ῥώμας ποτὲ θῆκεν ἄναξ[2]·
ἀλλὰ τότ' ἀξυνέτοις ἑρμηνέων
κάρτ' ἐχάτιζον ἐν ἀστοῖς·
ἦν τε νέφος βαρὺ δὴ λάθας, πρὶν ἐκεῖνος ἀναστὰς
εὐθύπορον στίβον ἐξαγήσιος ἀγεμόνευσ' ἀψευδέος,
παντὶ ἔργῳ κανόνας προφέρων
στάθμᾳ παλαιᾷ συμμέτρους,

τῶν τε πρὶν ῥήτρας ἀνέδειξε νόμων. οὐδ' ὀρφαναῖς   στρ. γ'
καρποῖο βουλαῖς ἅπτετο· τοῦ γὰρ ὄπισθεν
ἄλλος ἐξ ἄλλου διαδεξάμενοι, ξανθᾶς φλογὶ δᾳδὸς ὁμοῖον,
τόνδε θεμίσκοπον ἀθληταὶ πόνον,
ἄνδρας ἀϊδροδίκας
προδιδάσκοντες σοφῶς
ἆγον εἰς εὐκοσμίαν·

1 Irnerius (circ. A.D. 1080—1118), 'merito appellatus lucerna iuris, tanquam primus illuminator nostre scientie' (Diplovataccius ap. Sarti P. II. 263).
2 Iustinianus.

χρὴ δὲ παύρους γαρύεν ἐν πολέσι· ζεῦξον λύρᾳ   ἀντ. γ΄
τὸν χρυσέαις γλώσσας χαρίτεσσι κλεεννόν[3].
μηδ᾽ ἀοιδᾶν ἄμμορος ἔστω ὁ θησαυρὸς θεμίτων βαθυμῆτα
πὰρ προτέροισι κλύων[4], δισσοῖς[5] ἁμᾶ
τοῖσιν ἐπωνυμίαν
θέσαν αἵδ᾽ ἕδραι πυλᾶν
τᾶν Ῥαβενναιᾶν ἄπο·

πολλῶν δέ με καιρὸς ἐρύκει χἀτέρων   ἐπ. γ΄
μνάμονα, τῶν ἀπ᾽ ἄωτον δρεψόμενος πραπίδων
νίσετο πανταχόθεν πλειστόμβροτος
ἐς πολύκοινον ὅμιλος
ὀμφαλὸν Αὐσονίας· ξυνὰν μὲν ὄπ᾽ ἦλθον ἱέντες[6]
ὅσσοι Ἰαπυγίας τ᾽ ἐντὸς πυμάτας πεδίων θ᾽ ἵδρυνθ᾽ ἵνα
πλασίαν Ἄλπεσι γᾶν ὕδασιν
ἄρδει ταχυρρώστοις Πάδος·

[3] Bulgarus, 'os aureum'.
[4] Martinus Gosia, 'copia legum'.
[5] Jacobus de porta Ravennate; Hugo de porta Ravennate: quo cognomine significatur ea Bononiae regio in qua habitabant, cum quattuor priscae urbis regiones a portis quattuor maioribus nomina invenerint (porta Ravegnana, porta Procolo, porta Pieri, porta Stieri).—De his quattuor doctoribus, qui saeculo post natum Christum duodecimo medio Bononiae florebant, post alios dixit Savigny, Gesch. des römischen Rechts im Mittelalter, IV. 66 sqq.
[6] 'Citramontani' Universitatis Bononiensis discipuli, olim in Nationes septemdecim divisi.

ἦλθε δ' ἀνδρῶν ἀλλοθρόων ἀναρίθμητ' ἔθνεα⁷,   στρ. δ'
οἳ Γαλλίας ναῖον πλάκας, ἠδὲ Τάγοιο
πὰρ μελαμφύλλοιο ῥοαῖσι, πολύπλαγκτός θ' ἵνα κίδναται Ἴστρος,
οἷς τ' ὀρέων καθύπερθ' Ἑρκυνίων
εἰς ἅλα Σαρματικὰν
τέτατο στάθμ', οἵ τ' ἔχον
νᾶσος Ἄγγλων ἐσχάτας,

πόντιος τᾶν Ὀρσοτρίαινα φύλαξ οὐ λάθεται·   ἀντ. δ'
τὰς δή ποτ' ἐλθὼν τοῦδε γόνος πτολιέθρου⁸,
καλλίπυργος τοῦ φάτιν οἶδε λόγοις Ὀξωνία ἐν πολιοῖσι,
θεσμοφόροιο μερίμνας εὔσκοπον
σπεῖρε διδασκαλίαν·
ἕτερον δ' οὐκ ἄλλοθεν
ἄνδρα τεθμοὺς εἰδότα⁹

---

⁷ 'Ultramontani', ab omnibus fere Europae partibus Bononiam confluentes, quorum Nationes censebantur duodeviginti.

⁸ Vacarius, qui cum Angliam circ. A.D. 1140 venisset, iurisprudentiae studia Oxonii instituit.

⁹ Franciscum Accursii, doctorem Bononiensem, clarissimi glossatoris filium, in Angliam vocavit rex Edvardus I., qui a Palaestina rediens A.D. 1273 Bononiam devertit. Regis 'secretarius', 'familiaris', 'clericus' appellabatur Franciscus, qui decennium in Anglia commoratus cum multa ac gravissima negotia prudenter gessisset, in patriam reversus docendi munus Bononiae denuo suscepit.

δουρίκλυτος εὕρετο ποιμὰν Ἀγγλίας,   ἐπ. δ΄

εὖθ᾽ ἁλιερκέα πρὸς πάτραν Συρίαθεν ἰὼν

πὰρ σέ, Βονωνία, ἵκετ᾽, εἶδέ τε

μυριοπληθέος ἥβας

φῦλα τόπων ἀπὸ πάντων σαῖς παρεόντ᾽ ἐν ἀγυιαῖς,

ἀστυνόμοιο Δίκας σπεύδοντ᾽ ἀΐειν· σοφίας δ᾽ ἐξαιρέτου

φιλτάταν Ἡσυχίᾳ δύνασιν

θάμβαινεν αἰχματᾶν ἀγός.

οὐδὲ μάν, τὸν Φιλυρίδας ποτὲ θρέψ᾽ ἐν Παλίου   στρ. ε΄

βάσσαισι Χείρων, νωδυνίας γ᾽ ἕνεκ᾽ ἐσλῶν

τεκτόνων γυιαρκέος ἄστεϊ τῷδ᾽ Ἀσκληπιὸς ἔσχε τι μομφάν,

ἀμφὶ τομαῖς¹⁰ κλέος ἄλλοις μὲν πορών,

αὐτόματον δ᾽ ἑτέρῳ¹¹

συνέμεν νεύρων φύσιν,

τὰν θεοὶ κρύψαν πάρος·

---

[10] Mondino ('Mundinus'), qui circ. A.D. 1315 Bononiae docebat, humani corporis anatomiam in primis illustravit ; unde schola medicinae Bononiensis, iampridem inclyta, magis etiam celebrari coeperat.
[11] Ludovico Galvani.

ἐντὶ δ' οἷς Μαίας τόκος ὤπασε, Κυλλάνας σκοπός,   ἀντ. ε'
ξεινᾶν τε γλωσσᾶν κλαῗδας[12], ἠδὲ σοφιστᾶν
τῶν πάλαι γνώμας φράσαι ὀψιγόνοις· τοῦ[13] δ' ἔξοχος ἦν τότε φάμα,
ὃς μετ' Ἀριστοτέλει ἴχνη βεβώς,
ἀντία δ' ἐξενέπων
Ἄραβος κλεινοῦ φραδαῖς,
τάνδ' ἐκύδανεν πόλιν·

ἴστω δὲ καὶ ἄλλον ἔχοισ' ἐξ ἀρσένων   ἐπ. ε'
οὐκέτ' ἀραρότα κόμπον· δεῖξε γὰρ ἁ Κρονίδα
παρθένος ἐνθάδε πλεῖστον παρθένοις
οὐ πινυτᾶς φθονέοισα
φροντίδος· οὐδ' ἄρα κούρας[14] πάντ' ὄνυμ' ἐξαπόλωλε
πατρόθεν ἀμφιπόλου τεθμῶν, μελετήμασι[15] πατρῴοις ζυγέν·
ἄλλα τ' ἄλλαις μέλεν· ἦν δέ τις[16] ἂν
φωνᾶς κελεύθους Ἑλλάδος

[12] Mirae saltem loquendi facultatis caussa commemoretur Josephus Mezzofanti.

[13] Pietro Pomponazzi ('Pomponatius'), qui postquam A.D. 1512 Bononiam
venerat ibi librum 'De Immortalitate Animae' scripsit ; vir inter philosophiae
studiosos qui post renatam, ut aiunt, litterarum scientiam exstiterant idcirco
memorabilis, quod Aristotelis de anima doctrinam ad normam Alexandri Aphro-
disiensis potissime interpretans princeps ausus est Averrois (Ἄραβος) rationem
impugnare.

[14] Novella d' Andrea, A.D. 1312 nata ; cui pater Johannes Andreae, iuris
canonici doctor nobilissimus, praelectiones habendas interdum delegabat. Velo
ab auditoribus discreta virgo docuisse traditur.

[15] 'Novella in Decretales'. Id nomen libro suo posuit Johannes Andreae, ut
Novellae et coniugis et filiae memoria cum novitatis significatione coniungeretur.

[16] Clotilda Tambroni (A.D. 1758—1817), Josephi Tambroni poetae et historici
soror, litterarum Graecarum disciplinae in Universitate Bononiensi praefuit.

ἐξελίσσοισαν γλεφάροις ἴδε Παλλὰς μειλίχοις.   στρ. ϛ′
τίς πάντα κ᾽ ὢν φθέγξαιθ᾽ ὅσα τοῖσδε πολίταις
ἔργα λεύσσειν ἱμερόεντα βαθύζωνοι Χάριτες παρέδωκαν,
ἢ Παρίοιο λίθου σμιλεύματα,
κόσμον ὁποῖα τάφου
ὁ μελαμπέπλων λάχεν
ἱρέων ἀρχαγέτας[17],

ἠὲ ναοὺς πλινθυφέων τε μελάθρων παστάδας   ἀντ. ϛ′
ἐν Σειρίου θάλπει μαλερῷ σκιοέσσας,
ποικιλᾶν ἢ θαύματα πολλὰ γραφᾶν; θεῖος δ᾽ ἄρ᾽ ὅτ᾽ ἀνδράσιν
    ἔλθῃ,
τοῖσδε τὰ καὶ τὰ καλῶν ἄμφαν᾽ Ἔρως·
οἷον ἐφαμερίων
ἀρετᾶς συμπράκτορα
φᾶ τις ἔμμεν καρδίαις

ταύτας ποτ᾽ ἀοιδὸς[18] ἀν᾽ ἕδρας εὐκλεής·   ἐπ. ϛ′
τὸν καὶ ἑοῦ πατέρος τιμᾷ προσέμιξε σέβων
κεῖνος[19] ὃς οἰχομένων ψυχαῖς ἴδεν
κεκριμέναν τρίχα μοῖραν·

[17] S. Dominicus, in aede Bononiensi sepultus.
[18] Guido Guinicelli, poeta Bononiensis (circ. A.D. 1260), quem appellat
[19] Dante, Purg. XXVI. 97, 'il padre | Mio, e degli altri miei miglior, che
mai | Rime d' amore usâr dolci e leggiadre'.

δαιμονίοιο γὰρ ὅσσοις κάλλεος ἔμπετεν οἶστρος,
τῶν χθαμαλῶν λελάθονθ'· ὡς χά φρασὶν Οὐρανιώνων ἀμβολὰς
συλλαβεῖν μαιομένα βροτέαν
φόρμιγγ' ἀπέρριψεν χαμαί[20].

καὶ πεδ' ἄλλων σοῖσι, Βονωνία, ἀστοῖς Ἰταλῶν   στρ. ζ'
ἦν καὶ τόδ' εὖχος, χαλκοκρότοισι μιγέντας
ἐν μάχαις κτίσσασθαι Ἐλευθερίας κρηπῖδ' ἀδαμαντοπέδιλον,
ἀστραβὲς ὄλβου ἔρεισμ' Οἰνωτρίᾳ,
ὡς ἀπάλαλκε θεὸς
τὸν ὑπὲρ κρατὸς λίθον
Τανταλείου πήματος[21],

δῶκέ θ' ὁρμὰν ἀλλοδαποῦ καταπαῦσαι δεσπότου,   ἀντ. ζ'
σᾶμ' ἀμβοάσαντας περ' ἀμαξοφόρητον[22].
βᾶθι δή, Μοίσαισι φίλα, μεγάλων ταῖσδ' ἐν κορυφαῖσιν ἐπαίνων·
παισὶ γὰρ ὡς παρὰ κεδνοῖς ἄφθιτος
οὐ καταφυλλοροεῖ
τοκέων μνάμα, φρενῶν
ἄνθος αἰδοιέστατον,

[20] S. Caecilia, qualem ostendit Raphaelis Urbinatis tabula in Artium Academia Bononiensi servata.

[21] Cum Fredericus I. (Barbarossa) a foederatis Italiae septentrionalis civitatibus A.D. 1176 devictus est.

[22] 'Carroccio', malus celsus in plaustro vectus, taeniis duabus albis a vertice defluentibus insignis et Christi in cruce pendentis effigiem medius ferens, quo tanquam signo militari in proeliis utebantur Itali.

τοιόνδε τὶν εὐσεβὲς ἄγκειται γέρας   ἐπ. ζ΄

ματροπόλει παρ' ἀποίκων· οἷα Καληδόνιον

καὶ τόδ' ὑπεὶρ ἅλα πέμπεται μέλος,

οἴκοθεν οἴκαδ' ἔπουρον[23],

τηλεπόροι' ἀπὸ Κλώτας[24] Ἰταλὸν ἐς πρυτανεῖον·

φαντὶ δὲ καὶ Βορέαν ἰοστεφάνων ἀπ' Ἀθανᾶν ἁρπάσαι

τὰν Ἐρεχθηΐδα, καλλιρόου

παίζοισαν Ἰλίσσου πέλας.

[23] Ad exemplar Universitatis Bononiensis a Nicolao V., Pontifice Summo, A.D. 1450 constituta est Universitas Glasguensis, quam instituta ann. 1482 condita vigere praedicant 'per accepta privilegia matris nostre Studii Bononiensis, omnium universitatum liberrime'.

[24] Clyde flumen.

The Reign of Youth.

θνητῶν δ' ὄφρα τις ἄνθος ἔχη πολυήρατον ἥβης
κοῦφον ἔχων θυμὸν πόλλ' ἀτέλεστα νοεῖ.

SIMONIDES.

WHEN Youth from regions of eternal spring
On earth's expecting vales descended,
The laughing Hours, that round attended,
Proclaimed the Faery King.

With graceful vigour and elastic bound
He lightly touched the ground,
As though his feet could leave behind
The pinions of the wind.
His breath had Nature's fresh perfume,
His cheek her vivid bloom,
Rich as the roses that his temples crowned.

HBA ΣΤΕΦΑΝΑΦΟΡΟΣ.

> While yet the flower of Youth's sweet hour
>   To mortal man remaineth,
> Full many a dream and fleeting scheme
>   His light heart entertaineth.
>   *From* SIMONIDES.

Εὖτε κάπους εἴαρος ἀθανάτου   στρ. α΄

ἐκλιποῖσ᾽ Ἥβα κατέβα χθονὸς ἐς βάσσας γλυκείαις ἐλπίσι
    θαλπομένας,

αὐτίχ᾽ Ὡρᾶν δὴ χορὸς ἁδὺ βλέπων, κύκλῳ ποσὶν θείοις ὀπαδός,

ποικιλομάχανον ἀγλαΐας κάρυξ ἄνασσαν.

ἁ δ᾽ ἐλαφρῶν γονάτων ὁρμαῖς ἔκυρσεν εὐρύθμοις

γᾶς, πτέρ᾽ ὥσπερ κεν θυελλᾶν ὠκύθοος παραμειψαμένα,

πνεῖ δ᾽ ἀκραιφνὲς πνεῦμα, χροιᾶς δ᾽ ἄνθος φλέγει πορφυροῦν,

ῥοδινὸν ὥσπερ στέμμα κρατός.

A sceptre in his hand was seen
Wreathed with budding evergreen:
His mantle, as it flowed,
The vernal year's impictured beauty showed.

And, lo! from bowers and dells,
Where'er within their cells
The Passions lay entranced,
Swift on the plain,
His subject train,
The loveliest of their tribe advanced,
To keep the Faery Reign.

First, newly wakened by the breeze and wave,
The young-eyed Wonder sallied from his cave.
With step abrupt and wildered gaze
He trod the scene's mysterious maze.
Now he marked with coy delight
The sun all-glorious on the mountain height;
Now from the glancing rays
Withdrew his timid sight,
Again recoiling as the lake displayed
His unknown image, and across the glade
Moved, like an airy sprite, his lengthened shade.

σκᾶπτον ἐν χερσὶν φορέοισα πρέπει   ἀντ. αʹ

ἀμφὶ δάφνᾳ πλεχθὲν ἀειθαλεί, στολμὸς δ᾽ ἀγανᾶς ἀμφιχυθεὶς
    χλαμύδος

δεῖξε φοινικάνθεμον εἰαρινᾶς ὥρας γραφᾶν τέχναισι κάλλος.

ἠνίδε, φυλλοκόμων λιμένων χλωρῶν τ᾽ ἀπ᾽ ἀγκῶν

δαίμονες οἳ πρὶν ὕπνου θέλκτροις ἔκεινθ᾽ ὑπάκοοι

νῦν ἀνᾴξαντες ταχύνοισ᾽ ἂμ πεδίον, μαλακαῖσι θεᾶς

ἐντολαῖς εἴκοντες, ἀφθάρτου γένους ἔξοχοι,

κράτος ἑορτάζοντες Ἥβας.

πρῶτος, αὔραις καὶ ψιθυροῖς ὕδασιν κοίτας ἐγερθεὶς ἀρτίως,   ἐπ. αʹ

ὄμμασι φαιδρὰ βλέπων Θαῦμας μόλεν κευθμῶνος ἀπ᾽ ὠγυγίου

σπερχνὰ μὲν στείχων, δεδορκὼς δ᾽ ὥς τις ἀτυζόμενος,

θεσπεσίαις γᾶς ἐν κελεύθοις· ἄλλοτ᾽ αἴθονθ᾽ Ἄλιον ἐν κορυφαῖς

αἰδοῖ πρόσιδ᾽, ἄλλοτε δ᾽ ὄμμα τρέσαις ῥιπᾶν ἀπεῖρξεν,

φρίξε δ᾽ ἐν λίμνας κατόπτρῳ θ᾽ αὑτὸν ἄϊδρις ὁρῶν,

καὶ σκιὰν μακυνομέναν ὑπὸ δένδρ᾽, ὥσπερ εἴδωλον, πέτεσθαι.

But who the rapt effect can tell,

When Music met him with her speaking shell?

He saw—he heard the trembling chords obey

Her cunning fingers, and he hied away:

Till soon, o'ertaken by the tuneful spell,

Back to her side the unconscious captive stole:

Then, as awhile she stayed her sweet control,

On that strange shell, in playful mood,

He dared a mimic blow to try;

Yet still, like one pursued,

Had half retreated ere it made reply.

And when her touch drew forth a louder strain

By viewless Echo mocked from caverns nigh,

On every side at every sound

Starting he looked around;

And still he smiled

Of thought beguiled,

And starting looked again.

τίς δὲ φράζοι χ᾽ οἷα δαμεὶς ἔπαθεν   στρ. β΄

εὖτε Μοίσᾳ πρῶτον ὑπαντίασεν φόρμιγγ᾽ ἐχοίσᾳ ποικιλόγαρυν ;
    ἴδεν·

δακτύλοις ἤκουσ᾽ ἐλελιζομένας χόρδας σοφοῖσιν· φεῦγε ταρβῶν·

ἀλλὰ γὰρ ἁρμονίας ἐπαοιδαὶ δαξίθυμοι

δέσμιον ἀμφιβαλοῦσαι μῆτιν ἔφθασαν μέλος,

εἶρπεν ἀγνὼς αὖ παρ᾽ αὐτάν· ἁ δ᾽ ὅτ᾽ ἐπέσχε τέως γλυκερὰν

Μοῖσ᾽ ἀνάγκαν, αὐτὸς ὡς μιμούμενος κουφόνοις

φρασὶν ἔτλα φόρμιγγα πλᾶξαι·

εἶτα πλάξας, οἷα διωκόμενος,   ἀντ. β΄

εὐθὺς ἐς τοὔπισθε μάλ᾽ ὦχ᾽ ὑπεχώρει, πρίν νιν ἀντιφθεγγομέναν
    κελαδεῖν·

Μοῖσα δ᾽ ὡς καὶ μεῖζον ἔπεισε λύραν ψάλλοισα φωνεῖν, κλάγξε
    δ᾽ Ἀχὼ

φθέγμασιν ἀντιτύποις πέλας ἐξ ἄντρων ἄδαλος,

πάντοσε βλέμμα τρέπων πάσαις ψόφων διαλλαγαῖς

οὖς ὑπεῖχ᾽ ὡς δὴ φοβαθείς, εἶτα γελάσμασιν ἀσυχίοις

ἔπρεπ᾽ ὡς λύσαις μέριμναν, καὶ πτοαθεὶς πάλιν

κτύπον ἐπάπταινεν νέορτον.

Next, o Youth, to welcome thee,

Sport prepared his jubilee.

From thickets pearl'd with morning dew

He on impatient tiptoe sprang to view

With shrill uplifted horn, and called his sylvan crew.

Redoubling shouts before them sent,

Forth they rush from his greenwood tent

With their high-flourished weapons of merriment,

Thy circled throne to greet.

Triumphal in air

A standard they bear

With many a garland decked, the prize of many a feat,

At the sight, a transport showing

From the bosom fresh and glowing,

Through the bright eye overflowing,

Loose or linkèd hand in hand,

Mirth leads up her frolic band,

With obliquely darted smiles

Watching 'gainst invited wiles.

δευτέρα δ', Ἥβα, σὲ προσερχομέναν στέψοισα τιμαῖς Παιδία

ἐπ. β'

εὐτρέπισ' ἀγλαΐαν· θάμνων δ' ἐέρσαις ἔκθορε λευκοφαῶν,

δακτύλων δ' ὁρμῶσ' ἐπ' ἄκρων ὕψι κέρας λιγυρὸν

ἧρε καλοῖσ' ἴλαν κυναγόν· τοὶ δ' ἄρ' αὐλᾶς ἐκ χλοερᾶς σύμενοι

διπλῷ θορύβῳ βέλε' εὔφρονα πάλλοντες κυκλοῖσιν

σὰν ἕδραν, θύρσον τιν' ἄρδην δεικνύμενοι,

μυρίοις νικαφόρον ἐν στεφάνοις, μυρίων ἄθλοις ἀγώνων.

αἶψα δ' ὡς τάνδ' εἶδε Θάλεια θέαν,

στρ. γ'

ἄγαγ' εὐγαθῆ χορόν, εἴτ' ἀνέδαν εἴτ' ἐμπλακείσας χερσὶν ἔχοντα
χέρας,

ἔνθεον φαίνοισά τιν' εὐφροσύναν, ἁγνῶν θ' ἁβρῷ κόλπων ἐν ἄνθει

δέργματί θ' ἱμερόεντι δι' ὀφθαλμῶν φαεννῶν·

λέχρια μὲν βέλε' εὐθύμου γέλωτος ἐξίει,

εὐλαβεῖται δ' ἀνθάμιλλον πρὸς δόλον ἐνδιαθρυπτομένα.

ἃ δ' ἅμ' ἠοῖ πολλάκις ψαίρει τε λευροὺς γύας

ὄρεά τ' ἀμβαίνοισα πίνει

Health is there, that with the dawn
Climbs the mountain, skims the lawn,
Oft on nectar feasted high
Borne by Zephyrs from the sky :
Wit, that strikes with gay surprise,
Jollity, that grief defies,
And, loving every touch to flee,
The random-footed Liberty.
With half-shut eyes ecstatic Laughter
Almost breathless totters after ;
One hand holds her bending breast,
While t' other points at antic Jest.
Leisure, winding here and there,
Dallies hindmost, heedless where.

Thus, o Youth, to honour thee,
Thus they kept their jubilee.
Thus to greet thee all conspire,
All enchanted, all on fire,
As joys could never fail, and never tire.

Yet hitherward adown the vale,
Where murmurs float upon the scented gale,
Desire was now espied

νέκταρ ἐκπεμφθὲν Ζεφύροις διόθεν, ἀντ. γ΄

συμπροθυμαθεῖσ᾽ Ὑγίεια πάρεσθ᾽· ἥκει δὲ Ματὴρ εὐτραπέλου
    χάριτος,

ἃ φθάνει κομψόν τι λέγοισα, πικρᾶς τ᾽ Εὐθυμία κρέσσων ἀνίας,

καὶ πολύπλαγκτος Ἐλευθερία, χειρῶν ἄθικτος,

σὺν δὲ Γέλως ἔπεται βάκχειος, ὄσσε μὲν μύσαις,

πυκνὰ δ᾽ ἀσθμαίνων σαλεύει γυῖα, χεροῖν συνέχων ἑτέρᾳ

κόλπον εἰς οὖδας προπρανῆ, τᾷ δ᾽ ὁμοῦ δεξιᾷ

τὸν ἄτοπον δείκνυσι Μῖμον.

λοισθία δ᾽ εὔκαλος ἀναστρέφεται πολλοὺς δι᾽ αὐλῶνας Σχολή,
    ἐπ. γ΄

ἄσκοπος οἷ κε φέροιθ᾽. Ἥβα, σὲ δ᾽ αὔξων πᾶς ὅδ᾽ ὅμιλος ἄγει

τάνδ᾽ ἑορτάν, κοινὰ τιμῶν ὄργια γαθοσύνας,

πᾶς ἑνὶ κηληθμῷ τε θελχθεὶς καὶ μίαν ψυχαῖς φλόγα θηκάμενος,

ὡς μήτε τέλους ποτὲ μήτε κόρου ταῖσδ᾽ ἂν μολόντος

ἀδοναῖς. ἀλλ᾽ εἰσορᾶν γάρ φαμι Πόθον

δεῦρο βαίνοντ᾽ ἔνθ᾽ ἀσαφῆ πέτεται φθέγματ᾽ ἀμφ᾽ εὔοσμον αὔραν·

Wandering the lonely stream beside
With an unsettled air.
Behind him scattered blossoms lay
Plucked in his eager haste and idly thrown away.
For, light and fickle in the lack of care,
His visionary mind
Still pants for objects undefined;
And as, where'er he turns,
The wistful ardour burns,
Amid the peopled beams
Before him many a phantom gleams
In every varied hue;

Till, hailed in vain by his extended arm,
At some rude wind they take alarm,
And vanish from his view.
'Twas then a chillness on his bosom crept,
He gazed around, and wondered till he wept.

'Tis gone—the quick-forgotten tear;
For Hope, the beauteous Hope, is near,
Earth-delighting prophetess,
That only knows to bless.
Bright as the morn that rises to behold
Ascending vapours turn to clouds of gold,

πὰρ ῥεέθροις δ᾽ οἰοπόλοιο νάπας   στρ. δ᾽

ὡς ἀλύων οἰχνεῖ, ὄπισθε δὲ κεῖνται πορφυρῶν οἱ φθειρόμεναι
      κάλυκες

ἀνθέων ἃς δρέψε τε καρπαλίμως δρέψαις τ᾽ ἀπέρριψεν μάταιος.

ἄστατα γὰρ φρονέων, ἅτ᾽ ἀγύμναστος μεριμνᾶν,

φαντασίαις τε σύνεστ᾽ οὔτ᾽ οἶδεν ὧν ἐφίεται,

ἀλλ᾽ ὅποι δή κεν τρέπηται, πῦρ τι δι᾽ ἥπατος ἄτον ἔχων

δέρκεται μορφώματ᾽ ἀκτῖσι ξυμμιγέντ᾽ αἰθέρος

ὅσα βροτοῖς ἄμφανεν Ἶρις·

ταῦτα δ᾽ εἰ χεῖρ᾽ ἐκτανύσαις καλέει,   ἀντ. δ᾽

οἴχεται, χειμῶνος ὕβριν χαλεπὰν δείσαντ᾽, ὀνείροις ἶσ᾽ ἀφανιζο-
      μένοις·

ἔνθα δὴ ψυχρὸν φρασὶν ἦλθε κρύος, κύκλῳ τε παπταίνων ἀγάσθη,

ἔς τε καὶ ἐξέβαλεν δάκρυον· καὶ μὰν δακρύσαις

ὦκ᾽ ἐπίλασιν ἔχει· στείχει γὰρ ἁ καλὰ πέλας

Ἐλπίς, εὐφραίνοισα Γαῖαν μάντις, ἀεί τι φέροισ᾽ ἀγαθόν·

οἷα δ᾽ ἀντέλλοισα λεύσσει λεπτὸν Ἀὼς καπνὸν

νέφεα τίκτειν χρυσοφεγγῆ,

She dances on the plain,

As if her listening ear

Caught from afar a blithe inviting strain.

She courts the Future. Can he aught deny

To the simplicity of her bespeaking eye?

Between them Fays are on the wing,

And ever through the sky

To her the pledges of his favour bring.

She courts the Future, till successive Hours

In distant light array'd

Look forth from arches opened through the shade

That still is rolling round his misty bowers.

τοῖον ἔξεστ' ἐν πεδίοιο πόαις ὄρχημα λεύσσειν Ἐλπίδος   ἐπ. δ'

ὥσπερ ἄρ' οὗς παρέχοισ' εἰ φθόγγον αὐλῶν εὔφρονα τῆλέ ποθεν

ἐξακούοι, φαιδρόνου σύνθημα χοροστασίας.

ἁ δ' ἐφόδοις μνάστειρα σαίνει μαλθακαῖσιν τὸν προσιόντα
      Χρόνον·

πῶς δ' ἄρ', ἀδόλοισι παρηγορίαις ὄσσων μαλαχθείς,

οὐκ ἂν αὐτᾷ πάντα δοίη κεῖνος ἑκών;

καὶ παρ' ἀλλάλους διαπεμπόμενοι φροντίδων πτανὰς ὑπουργοὺς

οὔ τι κάμνοισ'. Ἐλπίδι δ' αἵδε Χρόνου   στρ. ε'

τοῦ προσέρποντος πάρα σύμβολα πωτῶνται φέροισαι πιστὰ
      φιλοφροσύνας·

ὧδε δὴ ψυχὰν θεραπεύμασι κηλαθεὶς ἀνικάτοις γλυκείας

Ἐλπίδος ἐρχομενᾶν ὁ μέγας κλαδοῦχος ὡρᾶν

κλᾶθρα τέλος χαλάσαι πυκνοῦ ζόφου καταξιοῖ,

δωμάτων ὃς νυκτιλαμπῶν οἱ κυαναυγέας ἀμφὶ πύλας

κἄτι δινεῖται· τὸ μέλλον δ' ἐκκαλύψαις, σκιὰν

θυρίδας ὡς κοίλας διοίγων,

One prankt with flowers

Her notice greets,

And seems to sip

With rubied lip

A chalice full of sweets.

The next with gleaming torch displays

Fair blissful scenes—yet most attracts the gaze

By signs that fill the mind with more than vision meets.

Each is welcomed as it lingers

With her kissed and beckoning fingers.

If one should haply rise

In less alluring guise,

Hope does but mark all cheerily the while

Another close behind peep o'er it with a smile.

Yet ah! with gloomiest tidings on his brow,

A giant wizard of the mountains, now

Pale Terror came; and, while with cowering mien

A spell-bound troop were round him seen,

τηλέφαντον φῶς ἐπιεσσαμέναν   ἀντ. ε'

δεῖξεν ὡρᾶν ἐξ ἑτέρας ἑτέραν, ὀρφνᾶς προκύπτοισαν περιβαλλο-
     μένας·

ἁ μὲν ἀνθῶν κόσμον ἔχοισα πρέπει, χείλει δ' ἄφαρ φοινικοβάπτῳ

μεστὸν ἐϋφροσύνας προσάγει πάσας ἄλεισον·

ἁ δὲ τόπους μάκαρας πρὸς λαμπάδ' ἀγλαὰν δοκεῖ

φαινέμεν· τοῦτ' αὐτὸ μέντοι πλεῖστον ἐπισκοπέοντι μέλει,

σάμασιν γὰρ μυστικοῖς μεῖζόν τι σημαινέμεν

φρασὶν ἔχει θαῦμ' ἢ κατ' ὄψιν.

τᾶν δ' ἑκάσταν, πρὶν παρεληλυθέναι, τείνοισα χεῖρ' ἀσπάζεται·
                                        ἐπ. ε'

εἰ δέ τις αὖ στυγερὰν δείξειε μᾶλλον σχῆμ' ἐπιτελλομένα,

τᾶς δ' ἀφροντιστεῖ μὲν Ἐλπίς, τᾷ δ' ἄρ' ἐπισπομένᾳ

ἄδεται ὡς σκυθρᾶς προκύπτει δῆθεν εὔορνις γελάοισ' ὄπιθεν.

πέφρικ'· ἀχόρευτά τις ἀγγελέων χλωρὸς πρόσωπον

νίσσεται, πτάσσοντ' ἄγων φίλτροις ἀφίλοισι λόχον,

δεσπότας παμφάρμακος, οὔρεσι ναῖον πέλωρ ἄκροισι Δεῖμος·

J. T.   19

His lips essayed dark mysteries to unfold.

But soon those quivering lips were locked,

And his glazed eye-balls, in distortion roll'd,

Betokened things too dread for speech

Or shuddering thought to reach.

The earth beneath him rocked,

When mixed with thunder and the voice of waves

From black unfathomed caves

Was heard a dreary cry,

That echoing seemed in other worlds to die.

Then silence reigned, but such as threw

On Expectation's front a ghastlier hue;

For, with a scowl of grim delight,

He told that from the realms of night

Unearthly shapes were crowding into sight.

When thus the magic work more fearful grew,

A wilder eagerness his votaries thrilled,

And, at each stir or sound

Above below around,

Shrinking they turned, or fell upon the ground,

λῦε κλαῖδας σκοτίων ἐπέων·   στρ. ϛ´

χειλέων δ᾿ ἄφνω τρομερῶν κρύος αὐδὰν πᾶξ᾿ ἄφωνον, λύσσα
    δ᾿ ἑλισσομένας

ὀμμάτων στρεβλοῖσ᾿ ἐμάραινε κόρας, ἄρρητα σημαίνων ταραγμὸς

ταρβαλεώτερά τ᾿ ἢ κατ᾿ ἐρευνῶντας νοῆσαι·

χθὼν δὲ σαλεύεται, ἐν βρονταῖς τε καὶ κλυδωνίων

βυσσόθεν φωναῖσιν ἄντρων ὀρνυμέναισι κελαινεφέων

μίγνυται λυγρά τις ὀμφά, τῆλε δ᾿ ἀχοῖσα γᾶς

μεθορίοις ἄστρων τε λήγει.

εἶτα σιγὰ μὲν βρόμον ἐκδέχεται,   ἀντ. ϛ´

τοῖς δὲ καὶ πρὶν προσδοκίμοισι κακοῦ χραίνει παρείας δείματι
    χλωροτέρῳ·

φησὶ γὰρ κευθμῶνος ἀπ᾿ ἐννυχίου μορφὰς ἀναθρώσκειν ἀφράσ-
    τους,

σκυθρὰ δρακεὶς ἐπιχαιρέκακος· δεινᾶν δ᾿ ὅσῳ κεν

μᾶλλον ἴωσ᾿ ἐπαοιδᾶν μαχαναὶ τελεσφόροι,

προσπόλων θυιὰς τοσούτῳ μᾶλλον ὁμάγυρις οἰστρέεται·

εἰ δὲ κινεῖται ψόφος τις γᾶθεν εἴτ᾿ οὐρανῷ,

τόδε τρέσαντες προστρέπονται·

Nor raised their heads till his behest was known ;
For he could keep suspended, as he willed,
Their sense and breathing ; by his look alone
Could give them wingèd speed, or freeze them into stone.

But hence, ye tremblers, hence away,
Flitting as shadows at the glance of day !
For who are these, that, next beheld in motion,
Come like the fresh resistless tide of ocean ?

'Tis Intellect, aroused as from a trance,
Intent by Nature's clue
To wind through labyrinths, where at each advance
Her unveiled secrets meet the courting view.

'Tis young Disdain, with smile half turned
On bounds his vaulting feet have spurned.

'Tis Strength that lifts his rampant form,
As he could ride and curb the storm.

οἱ δὲ καὶ πίπτοντι χαμαιπετέες, πρὶν δ' οὐκ ἐπαίρονται κάρα
ἐπ. ϛ'

πρίν κε μάθωσιν ἐφετμὰς δεσπότου· κεῖνος γὰρ ἔχει τ' ἐθέλων

πᾶσιν αὐτοῖς ἀμπνοὰς ψυχᾶς τε μένος πεδᾶσαι,

καὶ δόμεν, ἐμβλέψαις μόνον, τοῖς μὲν δρόμων κάρτος μέγ'
ἀελλοπόδων,

τοὺς δ' αὖ κρυόεις δαμάσαι λιθίνους. ἀλλ' ἔρρετ' ἤδη,

Φωσφόρου τέλλοντος εἴδωλ' ὣς, τρομεροί·

τίς γὰρ ὁρμᾶται στόλος, ὠκεανοῦ προσφερὴς ἁγναῖσι ῥιπαῖς;

φαμὶ λεύσσειν, κώματος ὡς βαθέος   στρ. ζ'

ἐξεγερθεῖσαν, Σοφίαν Φύσεως στίβον ἐξηγουμένας μαστευέμεν
ἐκπεράαν

συμπλόκων ὀρφναῖα πλανήμαθ' ὁδῶν, ἔνθ' ὡς προβαίνει μᾶλλον
αἰεὶ

δέρκεται ἐκφανέας τις ἔσω τεθμοὺς 'Ανάγκας·

ὄμμα δ' 'Υπερφροσύναν λεύσσω τρέποισαν ἐγγελᾶν

λακπατήτους ἀμφὶ βαθμοὺς ὧν ὑπερέσχεθ' ἀναλλομένα·

ὀρθίαν δ' αἴρει Σθένος ῥώμαν φυᾶς, ὡς λαβρᾶν

στόμια νωμᾶσον θυελλᾶν.

'Tis Independence, on a rocky height,

Free as the tameless eagle poised for flight.

'Tis Valour that has met the eyes

Of spirit-stirring Enterprise,

And watches for the prompted aim

At which to rush through flood and flame.

Yet these are but a herald band :

The crested Chieftain is himself at hand ;

These shall but wait

On his heroic state,

And act at his command.

He comes, Ambition comes ; his way prepare :

Let banners wave in air,

And loud-voiced trumpets his approach declare.

ὑψιπύργοις δ' ἐν σκοπέλοισι πρέπει   ἀντ. ζ'

στᾶσα Ματὴρ αὐτονόμου μεγαλόψυχος ζοᾶς, ὡς αἰετὸς ἐκτανύσαις

ταρσὸν ἀδμὴς ἰσοφόρον πτερυγῶν· Εὐκαρδία δ' ἐγγὺς πολεῖται,

Τόλμαν ἐγερσίνοον ποτιδερχθεῖσ' ἀντίπρῳρος·

ὡς δὲ διαυλοδρόμος βαλβῖδά τις προσίσταται,

πρὶν δραμεῖν τηρῶν ἁμίλλας σᾶμα πρὸς ἀνδρὸς ἀγωνοθέτου,

ὧδε πρὸς Τόλμας μένει σᾶμ' ἅδ', ὅπως ἀγρίαν

δι' ἅλα πῦρ τ' ἄπλατον ὁρμᾷ.

ἀλλὰ μὰν αὐταί γε πρόπομποι ἐοῖσαι φροιμιάζονται μόνον·

         ἐπ. ζ'

νῦν δὲ πάρεστιν ἄνασσ' αὐτά, κόμαις στέμμ' ἱππολόφου κόρυθος

ἀμφιθεῖσ'· αὗται δὲ κείνας σεμνοτάταν κεφαλὰν

ἀμφιπολήσοισ', ὦκα δεσποίνας πανάρχου ῥήμασι πειθόμεναι·

χαῖρ', ὦ γενέτειρα Θεὰ φιλοτίμων χαῖρ' ἀέθλων,

τοὶ δ' ὁδὸν λευρὰν προκόπτοιεν πρόδρομοι,

σαμάτων δ' ἐν πορφυρέαισι χλιδαῖς καὶ τορῷ σάλπιγγος ἄχῳ

He comes, for Glory hath before him raised

Her shield with godlike deeds emblazed.

He comes, he comes : for purposes sublime

Dilate his soul; and his exulting eye

Beams like a sun, that in the vernal prime

With golden promise travels up the sky.

Onward looking, far and high,

While before his champion pride

Vallies rise and hills subside,

His mighty thoughts, too swift for lagging Time,

Through countless triumphs run ;

Each deed conceived appears already done,

Foes are vanquished, fields are won.

E'en now, with wreaths immortal crown'd,

He marches to the sound

Of gratulating lyres,

And earth's applauding shout his generous bosom fires.

τὶν προκηρύσσοιεν ἐπερχομέναν.   στρ. η′

ἔρχεται· τᾷ γὰρ φιλόφρων ἀνέδειξ᾽ Εὔκλει᾽ ἐπαίροισ᾽ ἀσπίδα
    δαιδαλέαν,

ἐργμάτων ποικίλμασι λαμπομέναν θείοισιν· ὑψηλὰς πελάζει

ἐν πραπίδεσσι τρέφοισ᾽ ἐπινοίας, ὄμμα τ᾽ αὐγαῖς

εἴκελος Ἀελίου χρυσαμπύκων μετ᾽ ἐλπίδων

αἰθέρ᾽ ἀμβαίνοντος. ἕρπει προσκοπέοισα τὸ τηλεφανές,

εὔχεται δ᾽ ὑψηλόφρων πρὸς πάνθ᾽ ἁμιλλωμένα

χθαμάλ᾽ ὀρεινοῖς τ᾽ ἐξισώσειν,

τῶν τ᾽ ὀρεινῶν ἄκρα χαμᾶζε βαλεῖν·   ἀντ. η′

τᾷ δὲ συννοιᾶν μεγαλοπρεπέων ὁρμαὶ φθάνοισιν βᾶμα χρόνου
    βραδύπουν,

μυριᾶν νικαφοριᾶν δοκέοισαι πείρατα ζαλώτ᾽ ἀφῖχθαι.

δρᾶν γὰρ ὅσ᾽ ἂν νοέῃ, τάδ᾽ ὄναρ καὶ δὴ δέδρακεν·

δυσμενέων γέγονεν κρέσσων, μάχαισί τ᾽ ἐν δορὸς

ἄξι᾽ εἴργασται τροπαίου Ζηνός, ὑφ᾽ ἀδυλόγων τε λυρᾶν

φαίνεται στείχειν, κέαρ γενναῖον εὐφαμίαις

φλεγομένα πλειστομβρότοισιν.

He comes, he comes: his way prepare,
Let banners wave in air,
And loud-voiced trumpets his approach declare.

All ruder sounds, o Youth, were hushed awhile,
Nor had Ambition run his purposed race,
When Love at last appeared to claim thy smile,
And at thy side obtain the dearest place.
Leaving a diviner scene,
Where her dwelling erst had been,
By Zephyrs wafted in a pearly car,
To this sublunar element
Her gliding course she bent,
And came through vernal mists, emerging like a star.

But first, o Youth, that she might be
Duly trained for earth and thee,
On ambrosia Love was fed
In Fancy's charmèd bowers,
Where his wand her footsteps led
Through mazes gemmed with flowers:
Making earth to her appear
Like a higher kindred sphere.

ἔρχεται· λευρόν τιν' ἴτ', ὦ πρόδρομοι, τᾷδ' ἀμερώσοντες στίβον·

ἐπ. η'

εἶ', ἀναδείξατε μὲν σαμεῖα, σαλπίγγων δ' ἄφεθ' ὕψι βοάν.

ἀλλὰ μὰν ἄρσην τέως, Ἥβα, κέλαδος φθινύθει·

πρὶν γὰρ ἐκείναν τέρμα κάμψαι προσδοκατὸν κυδαλίμοιο δρόμου,

μναστὴρ ἐπιφαίνεται ὕστατος εὐνοίας Ἔρως σᾶς,

φίλτατός θ' εἷς δὴ τεοῖσιν στασόμενος

πὰρ θρόνοις· ὃς θειοτέραν προλιπὼν τῶν πάροιθ' αἴγλαν ἐπαύλων

ἐς πλάκας γᾶς ἦλθεν ὑπουρανίους,

στρ. θ'

ῥίμφα λευκοὺς σὺν ζεφύροισιν ὄχους ὑγρᾶς διώκων αἰθέρος ἐξ
    ἀδύτων,

καὶ διελθὼν εἰαρινὰς νεφέλας ἐξέλαμψ' οἷός τις ἀστήρ.

ἀλλ' ἵν' Ἔρως προμάθοι χθονὶ τίν θ', Ἥβα, συνεῖναι,

Φαντασίας ἐνὶ κάποις βόσκετ' εἶδαρ ἄμβροτον,

ἅ τέ νιν θέλγοισα ῥάβδῳ ποικίλον ἄνθεσιν ἆγε πλάνον,

γαῖα δ' αὐτῷ θεῖος ἤδη χῶρος ὣς συντρόφων

παρέχ' ἀνάμνασιν μελάθρων.

Yet Pity then, benignly meek,

With faltering voice and moistened cheek,

To Love revealed, that Pain and Woe

Had found a place below.

And as she ceased, from grove and distant rill

The sound was borne of Nature's plaint,

Melancholy, low and faint,

A whisper to the heart, when all around was still.

Love, scarcely breathing, bent her head

And listened till her colour fled;

But, as it mantling came again,

Her eyes all eloquent expressed

An answer to the mournful strain:

For they proclaimed that in her bosom dwelt

Softness ineffable, a power and will

To conquer Force, the fiercest Rage to melt,

To find a balm for life's severest Ill,

And lull the Sorrows of the earth to rest.

φᾶ δ' ὀκνηροῖς φθέγμασί τ' ἠπιόφρων   ἀντ. θ'

Οἶκτος, ὄψιν τ' οὐκ ἀδίαντος· ἀλάθειαν φράσω σοι **πᾶσαν**·
ἐπιχθονίων

ἴσθι Λύπαν καὶ βαρύθυμον 'Ανίαν συγκατοικισθεῖσαν αὐλαῖς.

ταῦθ' ὁ μὲν εἶπε· ναπᾶν δ' ἄπο τηλουρῶν τε κρανᾶν

ἀντιαχεῖ μεγάλα Ματὴρ ἄσημ' ὀδύρματα,

πενθίμου φωνᾶεν αὐδᾶς οἰοπόλοις ψιθύρισμα βροτοῖς·

ὡς λιποψυχῶν καταφὴς ταῦτ' ἀκούων Ἔρως

ἁπαλὸν ἐξάλλαξε χροιᾶς

ἄνθος· ὡς δ' αὖτ' ἤλυθε πορφύρεον, φαιδρωπὸς ὀφθαλμῶν σέλας
                                          ἐπ. θ'

ἀγγελίαισι βαρείαις ἀντέφλεξεν· δεῖξε γὰρ ἐν πραπίσιν

τοῖα νωμῶν κῆλα παμπειθοῦς ἀγανοφροσύνας

ὥς κεν ἑλεῖν ὕβριν βιαίαν θέλκτρα τ' ὀργᾶς εὑρέμεν ἐμμανέος

κουφίσματά τ' αἰνοτατᾶν ὀδυνᾶν θνατοῖς παρασχεῖν,

καὶ κατευνάζειν μαλακᾷ χερὶ χειμῶνα δυσκύμαντον ἄτας.

Thus Pity's influence o'er her soul

Heightened Fancy's rich control.

Love from Pity learnt the sigh

That saddens, but endears;

From Fancy learnt the rapture high,

That trembles into tears.

Each o'er her slumbers fondly bent,

And both their inspiration lent,

Like rainbow tints in dewy lustre blent,

As in a flowery cave she slept,

Where bees, that had from Eden strayed,

Its native honey to her lips conveyed,

And by the murmuring which they kept

About her golden hair,

Lured from the sky such visions fair,

As Eden knew when Innocence was there.

τοιάδ᾽ Οἴκτῳ μᾶλλον ἐπισπόμενος   στρ. ι΄

μᾶλλον αὖ καὶ Φαντασίας ὑποθάκαις παντοσέμνοις κῆρ παρέ-
    βαλλεν Ἔρως·

πρὸς γὰρ Οἴκτου τοῦτ᾽ ἔλαχεν, στοναχᾶν λυπρὸν μὲν ἱμερτὸν
    δὲ δῶρον,

Φαντασίᾳ δ᾽ ἅμα συνθιασώτης προσπελάζων

ἵκετ᾽ ἐπ᾽ ὀλβοδοτείρας ὡς βεβακχιωμένος

φροντίδων ὁρμάς, ῥοαῖσιν γείτονας εὐμενέσιν δακρύων.

κοινὰ γὰρ βρίζοντος ἄμφω τηρέοντες λέχος

χάριτας ἐνστάζοντι κοινάς,

εὐδρόσους ἀκτῖνας ἅπερ μιγάδας   ἀντ. ι΄

Ἴριδος· κνώσσει δὲ μυχοῖσιν Ἔρως σπείους ἑλικτοῖς ἄνθεσι
    κρυπτομένου,

χείλε᾽ ἰῷ τεγγόμενος γλυκερῷ πλαγκτᾶν ἀπ᾽ Οὐλύμπου μελισσᾶν·

αἵ θ᾽ ὅτε μειλιχόφωνον ὑπερτείνοντι βόμβον,

χρυσοκόμους περὶ χαίτας σάς, Ἔρως, ποτώμεναι,

θεσκέλων τοιόνδε μορφᾶν οὐρανόθεν κατάγοντι χορὸν

οἷον ἐν γαίας νεόρτου κἀμιάντου σταθμοῖς

ἔσιδεν Ἁγνεία σύναυλος.

Love woke, and moving with impassioned grace,
Attempered to the music of her thought,
She looked as one that trod the liquid air;
While, from some hovering angel presence caught,
Reflected radiance blushed upon her face.
Yet, as a lily droops with moisture fraught,
Soon by her own rapt consciousness opprest
At Pity's side she knelt with heaving breast,
And seemed to ask, in gentle grief,
If sweet illusion mocked her fond belief.

But Fancy near, in triumph mute,
Still round her waved his wings.
For though she courted Pity's lute,
And bade it speak of tears,
Of sighs and tender fears,
Yet would she stoop to kiss the strings,
As in their silver tone
The Spirit of her dream
Had told of bliss alone.
Her brow she raised
And upward gazed,
As if her soul on one exhaustless theme
Would fain for ever dwell:

ἐξεγέρθη, φροντίσι τ᾽ ἐμμελέσιν ῥυθμὸν συναρμόζων ποδοῖν

ἐπ. ι΄

θοῦρος Ἔρως ἐδόκει βαίνειν ἐφ᾽ ὑγρᾶς αἰθέρος· ὡς δέ τινος

δαιμόνων ᾄσσοντος ἐγγὺς ῥιφθὲν ἀπὸ πτερυγῶν

φῶς ῥοδόχρουν ἔστιλβ᾽ ἐπ᾽ ὄψει· λείριον δ᾽ ὄμβροισι βαρυνό-
μενον

ὡς κρᾶθ᾽ ὑφίει, μελεδήμασιν ἀρρήτοις δαμασθεὶς

κάμψεν ἀσπαίρων παρ᾽ Οἴκτῳ γούνατ᾽ Ἔρως,

ὡς ἐρωτῶν, ἆρα τάλας δοκέων ἐσλὰ προσλεύσσειν δολοῦμαι;

ἀλλ᾽ ἄναυδος Φαντασία πτέρυγας

στρ. ια΄

ἄγχι δινεύεσκεν ἀγαλλομένα· τὰν μὲν γὰρ Οἴκτου σαίνεν Ἔρως
κιθάραν,

ἀξιῶν νιν δακρυόεν τι θροεῖν ᾆσμα στεναγμοῖς σὺν ποθεινοῖς·

προσκυνέων δὲ φιλήμαθ᾽ ὅμως ἔμβαλλε χορδαῖς,

ὥσπερ ὀνειροπολῶν λεπτᾶς ὑπαὶ μελῳδίας

ἄλλο μηδὲν πλὴν τύχαν εὐδαίμον᾽· ἄνω δὲ βλέπων συνεχῶς

φαίνεθ᾽ ὡς ἐνθουσιάζων ἐν μέλημ᾽ ἀμφέπειν,

τὸ δ᾽ ὑπεσήμαινεν, ἀδεῖ

Then smiled, as bidding mortal tongues despair

That wondrous theme's entrancing power to tell ;

And still would sighs pursued by smiles declare

She felt a pain that spurned relief, and bliss too sweet to bear.

Thus taught to smile and sigh,

Love now to Youth drew nigh.

The conscious heavens o'er her head

Their blandest influence shed ;

And on the earth her very sight

Had all things waked to soft delight.

The Elements with mutual greeting

Gave sign that Love and Youth were meeting.

The balmy Air, with humming sound

And sun-kissed pinions quivering o'er the ground,

Calls verdure, fragrance, life and bloom around.

Smoothly the forests now

Their shaggy honours bow ;

And up from lowly nests in mead or glen

Ambitious warblers rise,

μειδιάσαις ὄμματι, θειοτέρας   ἀντ. ιαʹ

φροντίσιν θαυμαστοτέρας τʼ ἐπαοιδὰς ἀμφιβάλλειν ἢ κατὰ
     θνατογενεῖς ἐνέπειν·

καὶ στενάζων ἐν δὲ μέρει γελάων ἄλγος τʼ ἐμάννσέν τι παντὸς

κρέσσον ἄκους ὀχέων τε χαρᾶς οἴστρημʼ ἄφερτον.

τοῖα γέλωτος ἔχων στέργηθρα καὶ στεναγμάτων

ἐγγὺς ἦλθʼ Ἥβας Ἔρως· τοῖς δὴ συνέχαιρε συναπτομένοις

οὐρανός τʼ εὔφρον ποτιστάζων ἄνωθεν γάνος,

γᾶς θʼ ἀπάσας φῦλʼ ἰάνθη

εἰσάπαξ ὡς εἶδʼ· ἀνέμων δὲ ῥεέθρων τʼ ἀντίφωνοι κληδόνες
                                    ἐπ. ιαʹ

συζυγίαν ἐδέχονθʼ Ἥβας Ἔρωτός τʼ· ἐν δὲ φίλος Ζέφυρος,

ἡλιοβλήτοις διαιθύσσων πτερύγεσσι πέδον,

ἁδύπνοον βομβεῖ τινʼ ἆχον, τοῦ κελεύοντος χλοεροῖσι βρύει

βλαστήμασι πανταχόθεν χθονὸς εὐόσμοιο λειμών.

ἀσυχᾷ δʼ ἤδη δασείας δένδρα κόμας

νεύει· ὄρνιθες δὲ λεχῶν χθαμαλὰς ἐξερημώσαντες εὐνὰς

That task with twinkling plumes the dazzled ken,

Or lost in light convey earth's gladness to the skies.

Voices meanwhile from other spheres,

Saluting mortal ears,

With chime of song from land and ocean sent

Mingled their melting ravishment;

And this the lay, to mount and vale and shore

That each enamoured wind in tuneful concert bore:

'Turn, hither turn thine eyes, o Youth,

Love's choice ordained to be;

And haste to learn the blissful truth,

That Love was formed for thee.

Take her, that Love in thee may find

All that is imaged in her mind;

καρπίμοις ἐν πίσεσιν εἴτε νάπαις   στρ. ιβ'

ὑψόσ' ἐκθρώσκοντι, φιλῳδοὶ ἀμιλλατῆρες, οἱ μὲν τῶν ἐπιδερκο-
          μένων

ὄμματ' ἐκπλήσσοντες ἀμαχανίᾳ τοῖς αἰολόχρωσιν πτεροῖσιν,

οἱ δ' ἀφανιζόμενοι περιλάμποισαν κατ' αἴγλαν

πρὸς Δία τᾶς ἐπὶ γᾷ βάξιν φέροντι χαρμονᾶς.

ἐν δὲ τῷδ' ὀμφαὶ βροτείοις ὠσὶν ὕπερθ' ἐπινισσόμεναι

χερσόθεν τ' ἄχοις ἀοιδᾶς ποντόθεν τ' οὐρίοις

τακερὰ θυμοῦ θέλκτρ' ἔμισγον·

ταῦτα δ' ἀκταῖς τ' ἄγκεσί τ' ἠδὲ νάπαις   ἀντ. ιβ'

ἱμέρῳ ζευκτὰν στίχες ἐξέφερον πνοιὰν ξύναυλοι· δεῦρ' ἴθ',
          Ἔρωτι δάμαρ

μοιροκράντων ἐκ τελετᾶν προσιοῖσ' Ἥβα· μέγαν δ' ἴσθ' εὐθὺς
          ὄλβον·

σοὶ γὰρ Ἔρως διὰ παντὸς ὁμιλάσων πέφυκεν.

ἀλλὰ δέχου τὸν Ἔρωτ' ἤδη φίλον συνάορον,

ὡς ὁ μὲν τῶν σῶν θεατὴς γιγνόμενος, βασίλεια, τρόπων

πάνθ' ὅσ' ἐννοίᾳ πλάσαις ἱμερτά που τυγχάνει

τόσα παρόντ' ἔργοισιν εὕρῃ,

Take her, that Love to thee may give

What most shall make it life to live.

No sweeter prize can earth provide

To crown thy guardian care :

O take her as a Queen and Bride,

Thy golden Reign to share.'

R. KENNEDY.

τὶν δὲ τοῦδ' αὖ κτησαμένᾳ φιλίαν εὐδαιμονίζηται βίος, ἐπ. ιβ′

ἔξοχον ἀντιλαβὼν ζωᾶς ἄωτον. μηκέτ' ἐπειγομένα

πόρσιον θήρα γλύκιον κτῆμα κατ' αἶαν ἑλεῖν·

τοῦδε γὰρ εἰ θήσει προμάθειαν, νόμιζ' εὐαμερίας πατέειν

ὑψηλοτάταν κορυφάν. ἄγε δή, λέκτρων τε δέξαι

τόνδε κοινωνὸν θρόνων θ', Ἥβα, πάρεδρον,

χρύσεον χρυσοστεφάνοιο τεᾶς ξυμμετασχήσοντα τιμᾶς.

To Mary.

Early wert thou taken, Mary,
　In thy fair, thy glorious prime,
Ere the bees had ceased to murmur
　Mid the umbrage of the lime.

Buds were blowing: waters flowing:
　Birds were singing on the tree;
Everything was bright and glowing,
　When the Angels came for thee.

Death had laid aside his terrors,
　And he found thee calm and mild,
Lying in thy robe of whiteness,
　Like a pure, a stainless child.

Hardly had the mountain violet
　Spread its blossom on the sod,
Ere they laid the earth above thee,
　And thy spirit rose to God.

Sulpicia, ante diem memini te linquere terras,
    vere simul fueras conspicienda tuo.
ver erat hic etiam, nec, te fugiente, per umbras
    desierat tiliae stridere murmur apum.
germina florebant : rivus trepidabat eundo :
    arboris in ramo dulce canebat avis.
nil erat aprico quod non rideret amictu,
    quom te siderei transtulit ala chori.
Mors aderat ; non illa minis, ut saepe, verenda,
    nec veritae similis tu, neque tristis eras.
sindone sic nivea placide composta iacebas,
    lacteola in cunis qualis alumna iacet.
necdum etiam violae, montanum culmen amantes,
    vestierant gemma proveniente solum,
quom pia deposuit te cespite turba premendam,
    coepistique Deo iam propiore frui.

INDEX.

I. *AUTHORS.*

II. *FIRST LINES.*

For EU product safety concerns, contact us at Calle de José Abascal, 56–1°,
28003 Madrid, Spain or eugpsr@cambridge.org.

www.ingramcontent.com/pod-product-compliance
Ingram Content Group UK Ltd.
Pitfield, Milton Keynes, MK11 3LW, UK
UKHW030859150625
459647UK00021B/2739